Historic Oakwood
and Lincoln Park

PARK CITY PRESS

About the Cover. Carroll Hassell and friends at play in Oakwood near Springdale Avenue and Harvey Street circa 1915 while Oakwood was indeed a city. *Photo courtesy Jennifer Montgomery.*

About the Logo. The illustration for the Park City Press logo first appeared as a pen and ink illustration in the international literary journal *Golden Book Magazine* in 1929, and was drawn by John Alan Maxwell, a Tennessee artist who became internationally famous as an illustrator for Pearl S. Buck, John Steinbeck, Sir Arthur Conan Doyle, and other Pulitzer and Nobel Prize-winning authors. Maxwell was the great uncle of author and publisher Douglas S. McDaniel.

Historic Oakwood
and Lincoln Park

By
Douglas Stuart McDaniel
with Jacob Knox Chandler McDaniel

PARK CITY PRESS

© 2010 Douglas Stuart McDaniel and Faith Andes McDaniel.
ISBN 978-0-9800553-1-3

Published by Park City Press
Knoxville, Tennessee

For all general information, contact Park City Press at:
Telephone: 865-936-4533
Email: sales@parkcitypress.biz
Web: www.parkcitypress.biz

Library of Congress Cataloging-in-Publication Data
McDaniel, Douglas Stuart and McDaniel, Jacob Knox Chandler
Historic Oakwood and Lincoln Park
by Douglas Stuart McDaniel with Jacob Knox Chandler McDaniel

1. Nonfiction. 2. United States. 3. Tennessee History.

1 3 5 7 9 8 6 4 2

Printed in the United States of America.

Table of Contents

Historic Oakwood and Lincoln Park

Younger Than Springtime. Teachers Norma and Paul Kelley hold hands at the Christenberry Junior High School Y-Teen Semi-Formal dance, April 23, 1960. *Photo courtesy Norma and Paul Kelley.*

6

Dedication

Paul Kelley and his wife, Norma, met in 1955 while teaching at Christenberry Junior High School. For some time, the two kept their marriage a secret, but before long, students and faculty knew. After their marriage was known, Paul transferred to Fulton High School in the fall of 1959.

Norma's father, Roy P. Sawyer, operated a barber shop on Central Street at Burwell Avenue, next to Bailes' Meat Market. The Sawyer family lived in a small bungalow at 324 Atlantic Avenue, just east of Central Street. Norma crossed the stage at Old Knoxville High School in the spring of 1951 to receive the very last diploma ever granted from that school. Their sons, Michael and John, were born on Churchwell Avenue and grew up in the Oakwood community, attending Oakwood Elementary School, Christenberry Junior High School, and Fulton High School, where both were valedictorians of their respective classes.

Norma taught school for 32 years: first reading at Christenberry Junior High and then eighth and ninth grade English at Whittle Springs Middle School, then she became the librarian at Whittle Springs Middle School from 1963-1993. Paul, originally from McMinn County, taught from 1949-1951 at Christenberry Junior High School, then served in the United States Army from 1950-1952. He taught at Christenberry Junior High School again from 1953-1959. He taught English at Fulton High School from 1959-1965. He was principal at South Junior-Senior High School from 1965-1970. In 1970 he took a year's leave to complete his doctorate at the University of Tennesee Knoxville, and then served as principal of West High School. In 1973, he became Director of Instruction and later Assistant Superintendent for Instruction until 1982. After taking a year off, he became Professor of Education at Knoxville College, retiring from there in 1994. He was appointed to the Knox County School Board in 1991 and served continuously until 2004.

Paul and Norma's dedication to Oakwood-Lincoln Park is evident from their long service in the schools as well as in their service to the neighborhood. They have been a part of the Oakwood-Lincoln Park Neighborhood Association (OLPNA) since it was founded in 1979. Paul has served as president and board member for OLPNA for many years.

This book is a long-time dream of Paul and Norma Kelley. For over 10 years, Paul and Norma carefully researched the area at the Knox County Library's McClung Historical Collection. Through the persistence of long-time Oakwood-Lincoln Park residents Becky French Brewer and Harold Elkins, the Kelley's met Doug McDaniel, Becky's co-author from her 2005 book about Park City. Through the gracious support of the Oakwood-Lincoln Park Neighborhood Association (OLPNA), we were able to gain access to private collections of photographs, and we sincerely thank the neighborhood for their patience and enthusiasm. From an ambitious start around early June, 2010, additional research was quickly done, and through the efforts of many people, especially long-time and former residents willing to share their early photographs, we were able to put this book together in record time.

Dr. Kelley wrote Chapter Five of the book *Heart of the Valley: A History of Knoxville, Tennessee* (1976), about education in Knox County. The book was published by the East Tennessee Historical Society, edited by Lucile Deaderick. This Oakwood-Lincoln Park book has been Paul and Norma's vision, and because of their tireless efforts, it is a privilege to dedicate this book to them in honor of their many years of service to their community.

Paul and Norma Kelley, this is your book. And a community thanks you. Park City Press is honored to help you realize your dream.

The Kelleys. Paul and Norma Kelley in a family portrait with their two sons, Michael and John. *Photo courtesy Norma and Paul Kelley.*

See Rock City. Roy and Ethel Sawyer got a pass on the Southern Railway in the 1940s to take their daighters Bobbie and Norma to Rock City in Chattanooga. *Photo courtesy Norma and Paul Kelley.*

Prologue

This is a book about families, and about neighbors. It offers joy and memories, sadness, sacrifice, loss, achievement, and prominence. This is a book about the people of Oakwood and Lincoln Park. It is a testament not only to the resilience of people who have lived here for almost 200 years, it is also a testament to the strength of Oakwood-Lincoln Park, a modern-day, urban, working class neighborhood that has seen good times and bad times. But through this book, the people of Oakwood-Lincoln Park will again know a more complete and storied history of their community and be able to use this knowledge to strengthen the bonds of neighborhood and influence new generations of families who will continue to find a well-planned community, with tree-lined sidewalks, historic Victorian and bungalow homes with sweeping front porches and gracious parlors.

These future neighbors will plant gardens, paint their porches, work on their cars and their homes, and watch their babies be born in this neighborhood, feeling safe and warm in the knowledge that their's is a good home. They will continue to unite and work against the influences of crime, drugs, and transition that affect many neighborhoods throughout the United States. No neighborhood is perfect, but Oakwood-Lincoln Park is a proud and noble home to many. From its design as several well-thought-out, planned communities, to the ruggedness and affordability of the older homes it offers, Oakwood-Lincoln Park is becoming more and more attractive to individuals and families as a place to call home.

In that, Oakwood-Lincoln Park is not unique. Like many neighborhoods across this great country, its many residents seek a life of safe streets, ball games, ice cream socials, and school, church, and business activities that bring neighbors into fellowship with neighbors.

But make no mistake. While such aims may be universal, Oakwood-Lincoln Park has a very unique history, and the lessons of its past can still offer guidance and influence the path of its future.

This book can be summarized with one simple word: portraits. It is really two books in one, in that the early years of the area, from the 1820s to after the Civil War, do not benefit from the modern technology of photography. For this reason, the early chapters of the book are heavily narrative, offering descriptive portraits of some important early families.

The second section of the book, titled "The People of Oakwood-Lincoln Park," offers the reader a privileged, photographic view of this vibrant community from the perspective of the families who have lived here for over 100 years. Many of these photographs, from early snapshots on Brownie cameras to more formal portraits, illustrate life in Oakwood-Lincoln Park, and may remind readers that the more things change, the more they remain the same, from sittin' and standin' for a picture, to the all important Easter photos and class portraits.

During the summer of 2010, residents and former residents answered an important call and graciously shared their photographs, some dating back to the 1890s. Over thirty long-time and former residents sacrificed their time and shared important photographs and memories to make this book possible. The publisher would like to personally thank each one of you for taking the time, and would like to make a solemn promise to each of you that not only do the memories you shared appear here in this book, but that they will also be shared with the churches of Oakwood-Lincoln Park—so that future generations may add to this important history. Your families are remembered, and for your contributions, a community is grateful.

Part One:
A History of the Oakwood and Lincoln Park Areas

Her Last 245 Acres. At its height in 1860, the plantation of George Wellington Churchwell and his wife Sophia Moody Park Churchwell was more than 1600 acres. Outlined on this map in white are the last 245 acres Mrs. Churchwell owned in 1894. The Churchwell home was set back approximately 500 feet west of North Central, just north of what is today West Columbia Avenue. Superimposed on a 1935 aerial photo, in which some orchards are visible south of West Quincy. *Map produced by KGIS at the request of the author, based on a Churchwell probate map found by Cathy Irwin in the Knox County Archives.*

Springdale Farm: The Churchwell Plantation

On a hot August 12, 1864, Colonel George Wellington Churchwell died in great peace at his residence near Knoxville, according to Parson Brownlow, the circuit riding pastor turned newspaper publisher and governor of Tennessee. That residence was, by any measure, large. It was a farm, or as some called it, a plantation. An East Tennessee plantation is not all that much when compared to low-country plantations in Georgia or South Carolina. However, this "plantation," located two miles north of Knoxville, according to key historical accounts, encompassed at various times in the mid-1800s over 1,600 acres, 40 slaves, and a dozen frame slave cottages. For Knox County, that's a big farm, according to retired University of Tennessee anthropology professor Dr. Charles Faulkner, who has been digging around Knoxville civil war sites for over 30 years.

According to Faulkner, finding the exact location of this old plantation could have proven as difficult as finding the exact location of the much more famous Fort Sanders, which archaeologists and historians have tried, even with photographic evidence, to pinpoint.

But what if you could find a map of the old Churchwell place, buried in some obscure probate papers? What if you could find a narrative account—from a library in Illinois, no less—that described a visit to this plantation to purchase horses in the summer of 1843? One hundred and sixty seven years later, it is possible to paint a portrait of the old Churchwell plantation. The re-discovery of this plantation occurred in the summer of 2010, during research for this humble book about Oakwood and Lincoln Park.

Unraveling a Mystery

From an 1899 account by Harvey Lee Ross of an 1843 trip to Churchwell's farm (Appendix A), we know the farm was "two miles north of Knoxville." But today, if you wanted to find a farm that was two miles north of Knoxville in 1843, where would you start? Take a short drive from downtown Knoxville, up the likely road that would have provided access. No, not Broadway. Venture out Central Street and head toward Sharp's Gap. Adjacent to Central was the Jacksboro Road. A piece of it exists today as Cooper Street, over by Old Gray Cemetery.

In 1843, the Knoxville city limits stopped at Vine Avenue and Central, or today, Summit Hill and Central Street, in the Old City. As the East Tennessee, Virginia, and Georgia Railroad would come to town in

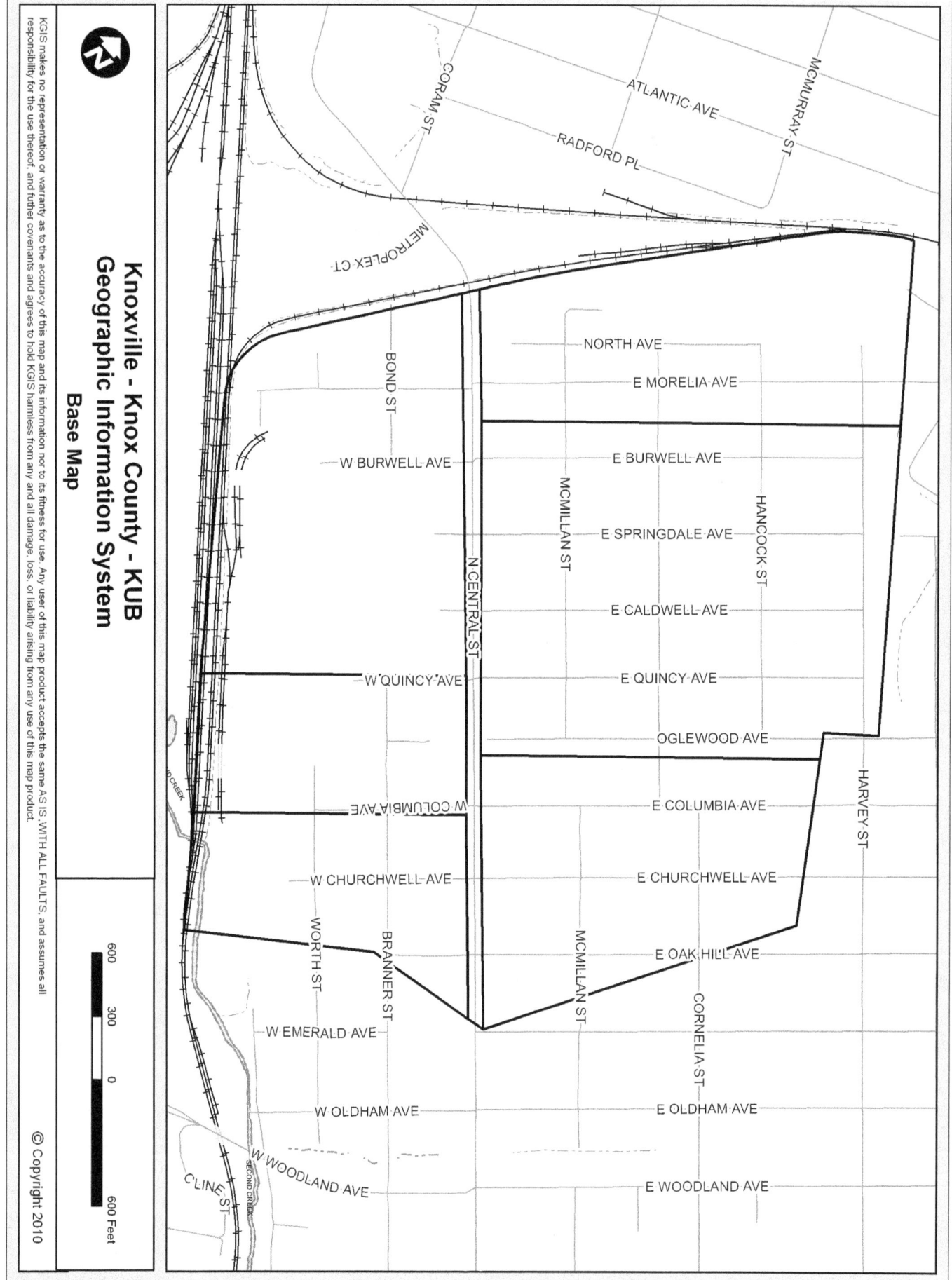

The following labels appear on the map:

MCMURRAY ST
ATLANTIC AVE
CORAM ST
RADFORD PL
METROPLEX CT
BOND ST
NORTH AVE
E MORELIA AVE
W BURWELL AVE
E BURWELL AVE
MCMILLAN ST
E SPRINGDALE AVE
HANCOCK ST
N CENTRAL ST
E CALDWELL AVE
W QUINCY AVE
E QUINCY AVE
OGLEWOOD AVE
HARVEY ST
W COLUMBIA AVE
E COLUMBIA AVE
W CHURCHWELL AVE
E CHURCHWELL AVE
WORTH ST
BRANNER ST
MCMILLAN ST
E OAK HILL AVE
CORNELIA ST
W EMERALD AVE
W OLDHAM AVE
E OLDHAM AVE
CLINE ST
W WOODLAND AVE
E WOODLAND AVE
SECOND CREEK

Knoxville - Knox County - KUB
Geographic Information System
Base Map

KGIS makes no representation or warranty as to the accuracy of this map and its information nor to its fitness for use. Any user of this map product accepts the same AS IS, WITH ALL FAULTS, and assumes all responsibility for the use thereof, and further covenants and agrees to hold KGIS harmless from any and all damage, loss, or liability arising from any use of this map product.

600 300 0 600 Feet

© Copyright 2010

Springdale Plantation. Outline view of Sophia Moody Park Churchwell's last 245 acres of the original Springdale Plantation. *Map produced by KGIS at the request of the author, based on a Churchwell probate map found by Cathy Irwin.*

14

the 1850s, the Knoxville city limits quickly expanded north to Jennings Avenue, on the southern edge of today's Old North Knoxville and Fourth and Gill neighborhoods. But in 1843, two miles north of Vine and Central puts you roughly near Springdale Avenue in the heart of Oakwood-Lincoln Park. Today, West Springdale Avenue begins at the Springdale Industrial Park, crosses Central Avenue and becomes East Springdale Avenue. It continues eastward to Harvey Street, just west of the ballfields at Christenberry Park.

But erasing the years of residential and industrial development, imagine heading up Central Street back in 1843. As it left town, before even reaching what is now Woodland Avenue, it became a rural road. After coming down the hill and passing by where the Rankin Restaurant is today, continuing a little further, you would have likely encountered a gate on the western side of Central, there at what is now Springdale Avenue. The Churchwell home was set back some 400-500 feet from Central. Behind the house, a spring trailed back to the southwest, towards a sharp bend in Second Creek that is still visible today. To the east, across Central where Oakwood and Lincoln Park are today, was a large stand of old-growth timber. Further to the west, behind the Churchwell residence, where the Coster Shop Yards are today, would have been stables for the race horses that the Old Colonel bred, and lush bluegrass pastures on which his horses fed. By the 1850s, the Churchwell's made a great deal of money selling the right-of-way across their land for the tracks that, by 1894, were referred to as the Knoxville, Cumberland Gap, & Louisville Railroad.

What is There Today?

*Where a plantation once was, the once-thriving but still very functional Springdale Industrial Park at 230 West Springdale Avenue is occupied by a number of small companies, that, while not harkening back in appearance to the antebellum nature of a plantation and often overlooked by passersby, would make any Knoxvillian proud of their respective industries. From metal recycling companies to the Gulf and Ohio Railroad works and repair facility, the area continues to chug along, and additional opportunities exist for light industrial development. Additional buildings at Springdale are available for development in 2010, from warehouses to crane-served heavy industrial facilities. This industrial park must be further re-developed if we are to realize the potential of new jobs and new homeowners continuing to revitalize the Oakwood-Lincoln Park community. The adjacent residential housing Helen Ross McNabb's new adult center is nearby, a beautifully landscaped facility. Unfortunately, the current emphasis for this area seems to be focused solely on additional social service industry, as Knox County Sheriff J. J. Jones has become the chief proponent for an alternative jail or mental health intake center at this location. Such a facility is likely to drive off potential private-sector investment in the industrial park, and it is not consistent with the I-275/North Central Street Corridor Study, published by the Metropolitan Planning Commission in 2007, and available at **www.knoxmpc.org.**

Similarly, the former Levis Plant, which once housed hundreds of workers at the Cherry Street Industrial Park in Park City is now a parole office. Such political decisions curtail or limit the potential redevelopment of these center city industrial parks and cost these walkable, sustainable communities important and very much needed jobs. We must not write off the potential for further industrial re-development, but consider the highest and best use of the built environment in Oakwood-Lincoln Park.*

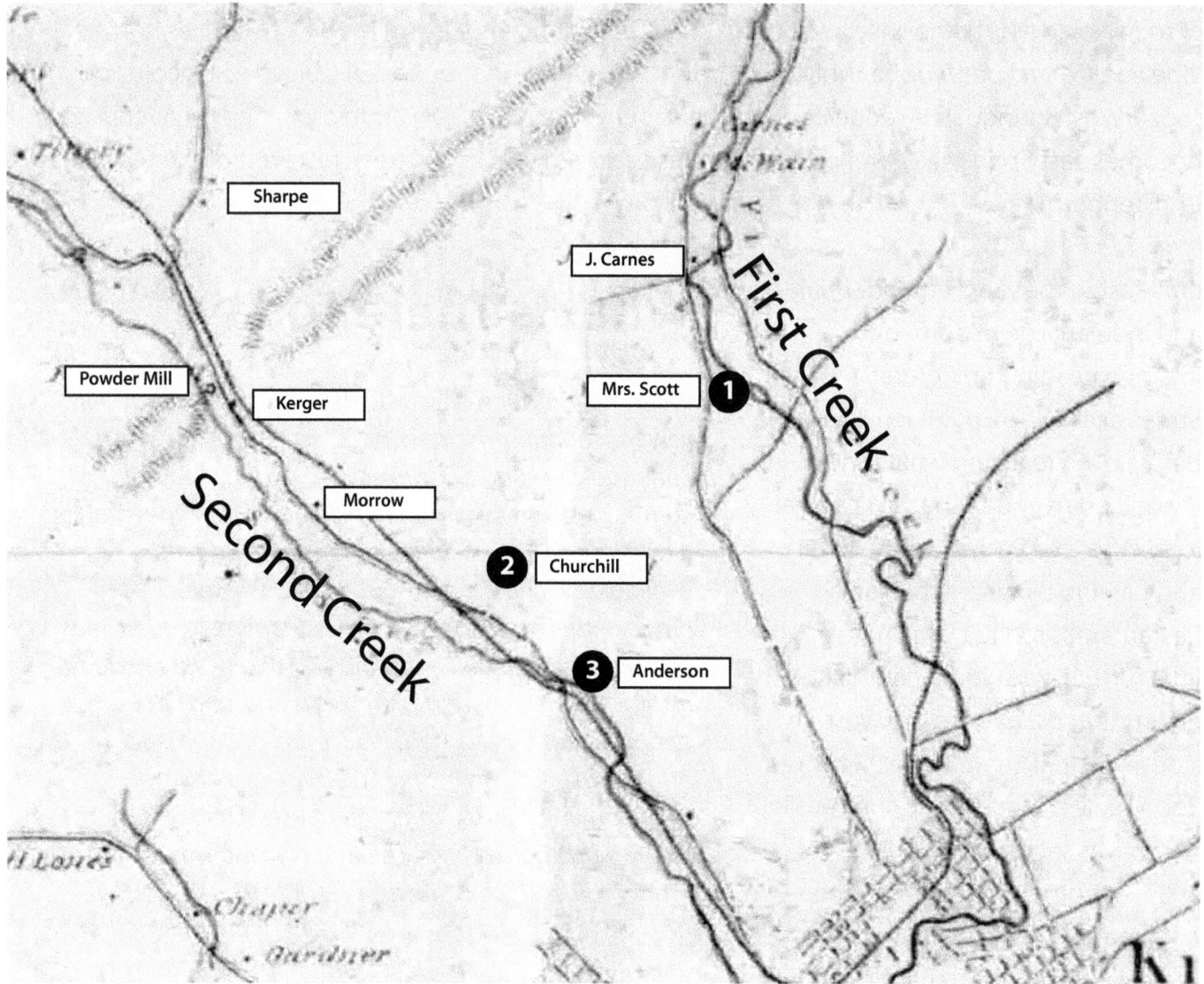

1863 Military Map of North Knoxville. Dr. Joan Markel, a PhD anthropologist at the Frank H. McClung Museum at the University of Tennessee, discovered this obscure map drawn by Captain Orlando Poe, architect of Union fortifications in Knoxville during the 1863 Siege of Knoxville. Labels were added due to the poor resolution of the map. This reconaissance map played a major role in allowing the Union forces to recapture Knoxville from the Confederate army. Markel discovered the map on a National Oceanic and Atmospheric Administration server, one of the least likely places one might expect to find a Civil War fortification map. Of note here is that this map indicates the location of at least six farms between Second Creek and First Creek to the south of Sharp's Ridge, including Mrs. Scott's place (1), the widow of Colonel James Scott Jr or her heirs, the Churchill (Churchwell) farm (2), and also the Andersons (3), in the approximate location of Happy Holler on North Central, as well as the Morrow, Carnes, and Kerger farms. Note also the Sharpe (sic) place north of what is today Sharp's Ridge.

The Anderson place further to the south of the Churchwells and Scotts (south of present-day Oakwood-Lincoln Park), likely belonged to the family of Alexander Outlaw Anderson, appointed U.S. Senator by the Tennessee General Assembly to fill the vacancy of Hugh L. White in 1840-1841. He did not stand for re-election. Anderson led an expedition to California during the 1849 Gold Rush, and served in the California State Senate 1850-1851, and the California Supreme Court from 1851-1853. He later practiced law in Washington, D.C., but died in Knoxville May 23, 1869, and is buried at Old Gray Cemetery. *Photo courtesy NOAA and Dr. Joan Markel.*

Colonel George Wellington Churchwell and First Wife, Rebecca Evelyn Montgomery Churchwell. Portrait of George Wellington Churchwell and earlier 1830s portrait of Rebecca Evelyn Montgomery Churchwell, mother of Congressman William Montgomery Churchwell, Rebecca Elizabeth Churchwell Charlton, and Laura Evelyn Churchwell Mabry, by painter James Cameron. *Photos courtesy Tennessee State Museum.*

Colonel George Wellington Churchwell

At only 33 years old, Colonel George Wellington Churchwell represented Knox and Roane Counties in the 21st Tennessee General Assembly in 1835 and 1836, according to the *Tennessee Blue Book*. He was then appointed U.S. Attorney for East Tennessee on January 18, 1840, according to the *Report of the Committee on Retrenchment of the Senate of the United States* (Gales and Seaton, 1844). The family likely and finally changed the name from Churchill to Churchwell in the late 1840s.

Colonel George Wellington Churchwell and his first wife, Rebecca Evelyn Montgomery, of Charleston, South Carolina, had three children: William Montgomery Churchwell, born in 1826, Rebecca Elizabeth Churchwell, born 1827, and Laura Evelyn Churchwell, born in 1833. According to records at the Mabry Hazen Museum in Knoxville, Laura Churchwell was born to George and Rebecca Churchwell in 1833 "at Springdale Farm," the Churchwell plantation north of Knoxville. This is likely the earliest reference to the name Springdale, a name that proudly lives on today. Laura would go on to marry General Joseph A. Mabry, Jr., the cantankerous Confederate general who would later be killed in a shootout on Gay Street.

As early as 1828—at the age of 26, according to deeds on file at the Knox County Archives, George Churchwell was already amassing large tracts of land along Second Creek, and was becoming a man

Laura Evelyn Churchwell. Daughter of George Wellington Churchwell and Rebecca Evelyn Montgomery Churchwell, born 1833. She married General Joseph A. Mabry. The Mabry home on Dandridge Avenue, known today as the Mabry Hazen House, was built in 1858 and is available for tours and special events. *Photo courtesy Mabry Hazen Museum.*

of importance in Knoxville: a lawyer, a successful farmer, and a breeder of fine horses. He also owned two important ferries across the river in downtown Knoxville, according to a 1990 article in *Tennessee Anthropologist* magazine. Citing JGM Ramsey's *Annals of Tennessee History*, the article makes some mistakes about the original ownership of the ferry in 1794, crediting it to Churchwell, despite the fact that he was not born until 1802.

Nonetheless, while the ferry had been in operation since approximately 1794, Churchwell was clearly a later owner, and the name "Churchwell's Ferry" likely dates to the 1830s or 1840s. Colonel Churchwell's two ferries were near the present-day Southern Railroad bridge and the Henley Street bridge. Churchwell also owned a mill on his land near the mouth of Second Creek at the Tennessee River. According to the article in *Tennessee Anthropologist* magazine:

> *Since various ferries operated upriver at different times at river mile crossing 647.8, the Churchwell ferry was known as the "Lower Ferry (Foster 1946). The crossing at river mile 647.8 was called the "Upper Ferry." Many early Tennessee riverside towns had "Upper," "Middle," and/or "Lower" ferries, depending on their relationships to one another." The area on the north landing in the immediate vicinity of the ferry crossing had been known as "Scuffletown" since about the Spring of 1791. The area was so named when a regiment of soldiers camped there spent their free time wrestling (or "scuffling). The Scuffletown tag was still in use in the 1840's (The Half Century of Knoxville 1852).*

Two sources—Churchwell's own tombstone and his obituary in the August 31, 1864 issue of Parson Brownlow's *Knoxville Whig and Rebel Ventilator* —both affirm that George Churchwell was only 63 when he died, August 12, 1864, putting his birthdate at 1802.

But who were the parents of this substantial Knoxville plantation owner and industrialist? Churchwell did have a sister, who he would visit in Illinois on numerous occasions. Born January 10, 1800, in Roane County, Tennessee, Harriet (or Harriott) L. Churchill married Charles Kirkpatrick in Roane County April 11, 1816. Harriet and Charles Kirpatrick moved to Illinois. See *Appendix A*.

According to genealogist Danette Welch, a reference assistant at the McClung Historical Collection, the only Churchwell in the Knox, Roane, Anderson Rhea, Monroe or McMinn County area who precedes George W. Churchwell and Harriet Churchwell is one Thomas Churchwell. Records from Wake County, North Carolina from 1795 to 1798 show a pattern of a Thomas Churchill or Churchwell, a tailor in Raleigh, as a defendant in several court cases involving debts. Thomas Churchwell was in Knoxville from May, 1800, until at least April, 1801, 10 months before the birth of George, but he departed the city suddenly, owing great debts. On April 13, 1801, Churchwell, who had been living with his family and servants at a home owned by either John Johnston or John Kain "removed himself out of the county privately, still owed for meat, drink, lodging, and other necessaries for Thomas, his horses, his servants, etc." While Johnston was owed for tavern bills, wine, beef, and sundries, he became enraged to discover that while Churchwell had sold a mare for $175 and another mare for $125, Churchwell had made no effort to repay his debts.

Welch found another obscure reference to another Churchwell in 1802. That year, an Elizabeth Churchwell served as a witness for the plaintiff in the case of Jessee Bounds vs. Bogan and Morrow (William Bogan.) She was paid $2 for serving as a witness.

By 1803, Thomas Churchwell is being sued in Gallatin, Tennessee (Sumner County) by Dr. Redmond D. Barry, a horse racing afficionado. While the parentage of George and Harriet Churchwell may be impossible to prove, the births of George Churchwell in Knoxville in 1802 and Harriet Churchwell in Roane County in 1800 do correspond to the travels of this Thomas Churchwell. If one were to hide from debtors outside of Knoxville, the remote and undeveloped Roane County of 1800 would have been a convenient place to hide.

However George Wellington Churchwell came to be in Knoxville, the man rose to prominence quickly, either through his own resourcefulness or perhaps through some wealthier patrons taking an interest in the young man. While maintaining his large farm two miles north of Knoxville, George Churchwell worked tirelessly as a lawyer, in addition to his many business interests which involved mills, real estate, and river ferry transport. He also raised and sold race horses.

Churchwell also maintained a healthy interest in politics. He was a close friend of President Andrew Jackson, at least through Jackson's first presidential term. However, based on the correspondence beginning on page 22, Churchwell may have indeed switched loyalties from Jackson to the short-lived presidental run of Knoxville's own Hugh Lawson White. White was appointed the US Senate seat by the Tennessee General Assembly when Senator Andrew Jackson became president (1829-1837). It was not until passage of the Seventeenth Amendment to the U.S. Constitution in 1913 that U.S. senators were directly elected by the people. Until that time, senators were appointed by the state legislatures.

Jackson's defeat of the incumbent John Quincy Adams in 1828 was seen as a backlash election. Jackson had beaten Adams before in the popular vote in the 1824 election, but Adams won by vote in the House of Representatives after another candidate, Henry Clay, threw his support to Adams. Jackson was re-elected in 1832, along with Vice President Martin Van Buren. But by 1835, the election of 1836 was already brewing over disenchantment with Jackson's tendency to overreach in his use of executive powers. Like incumbent vice president George H. W. Bush succeeding Ronald Reagan in 1988, the 1836 election would see vice president and Democrat Martin Van Buren succeed the retiring Andrew Jackson, but not before Knoxville's own Hugh Lawson White would also mount a presidential campaign as a Whig, or National Republican, with John Tyler as his running mate. Two other Whigs running for president that year would be William Henry Harrison, from the west, and Daniel Webster of Massachusetts. Van Buren received 50.8% of the vote, while Harrison garnered 36.6%. White came in a distant third, with only 9.7% of the vote. The Whigs, a political party begun in 1833, would continue in opposition to the Democratic Party until 1856. Whig presidents would include William Henry Harrison, Zachary Taylor, John Tyler, and Millard Fillmore. They opposed autocratic rule, and were in fact the "original party of Lincoln," as Lincoln was an early Whig leader in Illinois.

George and Sophia Moody Churchwell. The graves of George Wellington Churchwell and his second wife, Sophia Moody Park Churchwell lies close to the entrance to Old Gray Cemetery. Saint John's Lutheran Church, constructed in 1888, is visible in the background. *Photo courtesy Park City Press.*

The high drama of political intrigue in Washington during this time is illustrated in these two letters from White to his friend George W. Churchwell, first published in 1920 in *Andrew Jackson and Early Tennessee History Illustrated*, by Samuel Gordon Heiskell. The first clearly displays White's frustration with Jackson, who he calls "my old friend (who) is in open disregard of the leading measures he professed to entertain when he sought power..."

Senate Chamber, February 23, 1836.

My dear Sir: Your favor under date of the 8th instant was received, apparently safe, on yesterday. We have had, almost constantly, a state of very high excitement in Congress, and have as yet done but little, except talk.

The Globe *has become more and more abusive. It is now plainly seen that I will neither be coaxed, nor driven from the position in which I have been placed by my political friends. The only alternative, therefore, is to destroy me if possible. I am charged with insincerity, duplicity, falsehood, suppressing the truth, etc., without stint. In addition, it is obvious the whole power and patronage of the executive is brought to bear. For all this, I care not. My leading friends here stand firm, and fearlessly do their duty. How many of them may do so elsewhere, time alone will show.*

I shall calmly, coolly, and without faltering, as well as I am able, discharge what I think the duty assigned me, without stopping to consider whether it will elevate or depress me in public opinion.

The policy is to whistle off as many of my friends as possible, and to sacrifice the rest.

When the contest is over, even if left a private citizen, I would not exchange either feelings or character with the venerable Chief Magistrate. I intend to act, as far as God may enable me, upon the principles which I have ever avowed, which I believe are sound and correct. I will, therefore, have my own approbation: whereas, my old friend is in open disregard of the leading measures he professed to entertain when he sought power, and is saying, and countenancing others in saying, things against me, which he has the strongest reasons to believe are unjust and unfounded.

Our French War is happily ended. Should the instructing, expunging resolutions have passed, I shall leave for home as soon as I can take the necessary preparations.

If permitted to remain here, I have no doubt we shall have the names of some of Our Flying Squad in Tennessee before the the Senate for their pay. My health continues very good.

Most sincerely and truly,
Hu. L. White.

In the second letter to Colonel Churchwell on the next page, White comments on the political pressure and influence the Jackson administration is bringing to bear, both on White personally and politically to make sure that Van Buren, Jackson's choice for his successor, would be elected. White further makes a prediction: that even if Jackson is successful in getting Van Buren elected, the former president would find himself with few friends.

Hon. G. W. Churchwell.
Washington, June 18th, 1836.

My dear Sir: I thank you most sincerely for your letter enclosed to Mr. Lea, and which he handed me on yesterday.

I see no reason to conclude that anything which has occurred here during the session can have the effect of doing us harm; on the contrary, I think we may well flatter ouselves that progress has been made in giving to the people some useful information.

Everything in the power of the executive to do for the purpose of injuring me has been done, and I doubt not the same course will be continued.

In conformity with my own judgment, as well as what I believe the wishes of my constituents, I have in every instance sustained the executive, excepting only in such measures as I believe inconsistent with the great principles for which we all struggled when the present President came into power.

Strange as it may seem, I have no doubt the truth is, the President is exceedingly anxious that it should be known that his successor will have been elected by his means and influence; and I am perfectly convinced he intends to put down every man who dares to throw any obstacles in his way.

That the timid and calculating will yield to his wishes is according to the common course of things; as to myself I am content to await the result without anxiety. I will never yield to the dictation of any one man living, but will willingly chide the expressed will of a majority, be that what it may. That the patronage of the government has been used, is now being used, and will continue to be used to influence public opinion, I firmly believe. After the 4th March, 1837, the opinion and influence of General Jackson will be regulated entirely by the manner in which his whole public conduct shall be estimated by the community at large.

I venture one prediction, and that is that if he ever after that period should need friends, he will find very few among those he is now serving most zealously.

Why should we try to prove our letters were broken? Who cares? Those who are profited by such villainy will only be the better pleased. All we can do in such cases is to state the truth as it is, whenever and wherever we please, and let others believe or disbelieve us as best suits them.

You must expect and so you will find the truth to be, that you will have the opposition and enmity of all those who believe you are, or will be, in their way; and you will have better luck than I if you do not find those most bitter whom you have treated best.

Patience and good temper under injustice is always the best policy. When people lie, live them down by exemplary conduct.

Your letter at the close of the session was received and answered. As you did not receive the answer, some one else received the benefit of it.

If ill usage could disgust any one with the world I ought to be disgusted; but I am not. When those who ought to treat me well, ill use me, I am more than compensated by the friendship and support of those who are under no obligation to me.

Most sincerely and truly yours,
Hu. L. White

When Churchwell died in 1864, he was 63, and "one of the oldest and best citizens of Knoxville," according to Parson Brownlow's newspaper, the *Knoxville Whig and Rebel Ventilator*. Churchwell was a gifted attorney, and was for sometime the United States Attorney for the District of East Tennessee. He was also a Knox County representative to the Tennessee state legislature.

Churchwell was also a deeply religious man. While his second wife, Sophia Moody Park Churchwell, or Aunt Moody, as she was called by her step-children, was a devout Presbyterian, Colonel Churchwell remained a staunch Methodist, if not a contrary one. Aunt Moody not only influenced Andrew Jackson to become a Presbyterian, she also helped convince him to forgive his enemies.

According to Churchwell's obituary, "though he always expressed great dissatisfaction with his own religious charter and experience...in the latter part of life he seemed to be at perfect peace with God and all mankind. He expressed the greatest gratitude for deep and long afflictions, alleging that it had given him time and opportunity to see and repent of his sins and through atonement, to obtain pardon and peace with God."

Those who visited him in his remaining few weeks that summer enjoyed visiting the afflicted old colonel, who many years before had participated in the legal actions related to the removal of the Cherokee to Oklahoma. Perhaps it was these sins he felt the need to atone for, as those visitors would later relate that they were "more than repaid for the trouble and labor of the visit."

The old man surely had regrets. Whether due to age or infirmity, he may have been able to avoid taking sides in the still ongoing Civil War, but Aunt Moody had been suffering the devastation of her plantation by the occupation of Union forces. In addition, the old colonel had just witnessed the decline and fall of his young son, William Montgomery Churchwell, a Knoxville lawyer and banker who had been the two-term U.S. second district Congressman, working for a compromise to preserve the Union during his years in Washington, but ultimately siding with the Confederacy. The younger Churchwell was appointed Provost Marshal for the district of Tennessee in April, 1862 by Confederate President Jefferson Davis. Four months later, he was dead from typhoid, likely contracted from other Confederate soldiers during the previous year he spent in command at Cumberland Gap.

But whether suffering from physical affliction or deep remorse two years after his accomplished son's death, he didn't seem to let the suffering get him down. "Let me die the death of the righteous, and let my last end be like his." Whether he meant Jesus or his son William, we may never know.

George and Sophia Moody Churchwell. Closeup of the tombstone of Colonel George Churchwell and Aunt Moody Churchwell at Old Gray Cemetery. George, born June 22, 1802, died August 12, 1864. Aunt Moody, born June 5, 1817, died May 7, 1898. *Photo courtesy Park City Press.*

Ol' Rebel: Aunt Moody

Rebecca Churchwell, the mother of George, Laura, and Rebecca, died suddenly in 1834, possibly in childbirth. The young George Wellington Churchwell, the father of three children, quickly remarried. On September 14, 1836, he married Sophia Moody Park, born in 1817 to William and

Jane Crozier Armstrong Park. She was the granddaughter of noted Knoxville merchant James Park and his wife Sophia Moody (Park). She also had a first cousin with the same name, Sophia Moody Park, who would marry George M. White, Knox County Sheriff and an investor in the Edgewood Land & Improvement Company, a key developer of the future Lincoln Park.

While she had no children of her own, "Aunt Moody," as she was called, would survive the Civil War and the death of her husband, the Reconstruction Period, and like many of her Park family, live well past the age of 80. Aunt Moody is an important figure in the history of Oakwood-Lincoln Park because it is she who sold C. B. Atkin the original land which he developed into the City of Oakwood around 1905.

> **Aunt Moody was a force of nature and an unrepentant Confederate with a soft heart whom Union soldiers encamped on her North Knoxville plantation would call "Ol' Rebel."**
>
> **For a complete narrative account of Aunt Moody, told by a family member, please see Appendix A in the back of this book.**

Aunt Moody was a force of nature and an unrepentant Confederate with a soft heart whom Union soldiers encamped on her North Knoxville plantation would call "Ol' Rebel." For a complete narrative account of Aunt Moody, told by a family member, please see *Appendix A* in the back of this book.

Cathy E. Irwin, who now works at the University of Tennessee in the Department of Social Work, wrote her master's thesis at Ball State University on the suburbanization of Park City and Lincoln Park. In addition to sharing her thesis, Irwin also helped this author by tracking down a valuable probate map that was referenced in her will. The will of Sophia Moody Park Churchwell (Sophia M. Churchwell) was probated in 1898. Filed with it was a map. Using this map, the author paid to have it correlated to present day map information by Garrett McKinney of the Knoxville-Knox County Geographical Information System (KGIS). These modern maps (pages 12 and 14) clearly show the location of the Churchwell family residence—and represent the last 245 acres of the sprawling Springdale Farm.

Col. Churchwell's wife was also well acquainted with (President Andrew) Jackson, and knew him at the time when he was converted and united with the Presbyterian church, and had sat at the communion table with him, herself being a Presbyterian...She told us about what a time the minister had had with him to get him to agree to forgive his enemies when he was about to join the church. He told the minister that he was willing to forgive all his political enemies, but his enemies that had been guilty of defaming his private character and his wife, and of lying about his mother, he did not think he could forgive. But the minister told him that if he expected to have his sins forgiven he would have to forgive his enemies, and pointed him to many passages of scripture that treated on that subject. So the general finally agreed to forgive his enemies and was received as a member of the Presbyterian church.

Harvey Lee Ross, 1899

Perhaps surprisingly, the farmhouse was west of Central Avenue, but the massive farm encompassed land from what is today the Norfolk Southern Rail lines that lead north out of Knoxville, as well as the land that was the Coster Shop railyards, now partially occupied by Sysco Knoxville, a major food distribution center providing more than 300 jobs to the area. This Sysco facility serves Eastern Tennessee, Western North Carolina, Southeastern Kentucky, and Southern West Virginia. The Churchwell farm also included large tracts of land east of Central Avenue in present day Oakwood-Lincoln Park —as far east as Harvey Street. By 1894, the farm was reduced to a scant 245 acres. But Aunt Moody had done quite well, with an estate of $78,000 in cash, large amounts of property which she subdivided and designated her nephew, William P. Armstrong, to distribute among her heirs. During her lifetime, she frequently loaned money for investment purposes to friends and family.

Sometimes the historical researcher has to go away from the actual geographic area of study to find all the information relevant to the task at hand. In this case, it takes a 111 year old book about early pioneers of Illinois to learn more about that Churchwell farm "two miles north of Knoxville."

Appendix A of this book, *A Trip to Churchwell's Farm*, is an excerpt from *The Early Pioneers and Pioneer Events of the State of Illinois*, published by Harvey Lee Ross (1817-1907) in 1899, about a trip he personally took from his farm in Illinois in 1843, twenty years before the Siege of Knoxville, to purchase horses from Colonel George W. Churchwell at his farm "two miles north of Knoxville." This account provides much of the supporting facts about the Churchwell family, including George Churchwell's relationship to Harriet Churchwell Kirkpatrick.

The narrative, published in 1899 when Ross was 81 years old, is surprisingly readable, and describes in exacting detail Ross's trip south, his visit with Andrew Jackson at the Hermitage, only two years before the former president's death. It details such ancedotes as Jackson showing Ross through his apple orchards, taking apples to Jackson's good friends, the Churchwells, and even describes Sophia Moody Park Churchwell's involvement in converting Jackson to a Presbyterian. Further, it graphically describes the Churchwell plantation north of Knoxville, including their slaves, how they treated them, and how they entertained their cousins with a slave "corn shucking and dance." That this account describes life on a plantation that is now the area known as Oakwood and Lincoln Park offers the reader an incredibly rare glimpse into antebellum Knoxville history. Chronological references such as "as I told you last week" imply that Mr. Ross's accounts were likely serialized in a weekly column in the Fulton County, Illinois newspaper when this was originally published in 1899.

Of greater import here is the story of how Colonel George Churchwell and "Aunt Moody" Churchwell regularly traveled to Illinois to visit these cousins. What is revealed is an account of their last visit to Illinois in 1856, when a young cousin, Frank Ross, then about 10 years old, promises Aunt Moody that he will visit Tennessee when he is grown. About eight years later, now a member of the 84th Illinois Regiment, he is deployed at a Union encampment located on the very Churchwell plantation that he promised Aunt Moody he would one day visit. He is summoned to "headquarters," the Churchwell home, where Aunt Moody is chastising the commander of the regiment, Colonel Louis Waters (another personal friend of Abraham Lincoln) for the continued devastation to her plantation. She finally asks where these boys are from, and Colonel Waters informs her that they are from Illinois. She asks if there are Kirkpatricks or Ross's in their unit, her cousins from Illinois. Indeed, a young Frank Ross is killing and frying her chickens down near Second Creek, likely near that sharp bend in the creek. She warns Colonel Waters to take care of the lad, and that if he is injured, to make sure that they bring Frank, a Union soldier, straight to her.

As part of Longstreet's forces, Colonel Waters was approaching Cleveland, Tennessee in February, 1864, after the Siege of Knoxville of November, 1863, when Union forces re-captured Knoxville in a short but horrendous battle in which heavy Confederate losses were encountered. The Confederates retreated through the neighborhoods of North Knoxville, and it is likely that Colonel Waters unit was encamped at the Churchwell plantation by late summer or early fall, 1864. This would explain why Colonel Churchwell himself is not mentioned in the account, as he died August 12, 1864. Aunt Moody Churchwell became the owner of the plantation, and was still there in 1880, according to census data, when she lived there with her sister, Ann E. Armstrong, Ann's son Robert, age 35, and five African American laborers or servants, including Abe Anderson, age 65, a "black laborer," Ellen Johnson, age

45, a "black servant," Robert Johnson, her 15 year old son, and Lavine Smith, a 26 year-old female "black servant" and her 10 year old son, John. In the 1870 census, just after the war, the estate was valued at only $25,000, and Ellen Johnson was older—58, a "black cook" and Ellen's three children Fanny, age 12, Kitty, age 8, and Bob, age 5, lived with Mrs. Churchwell. Only 10 years earlier, before the war and before Colonel Churchwell's death, the combined value of Colonel and Mrs. Churchwell's real estate was $113,000, and their personal property, which would have included the monetary value of their slaves, was $30,000.

Sophia Moody Park Churchwell is buried with her husband, Colonel George Wellington Churchwell, at Old Gray Cemetery on Broadway. As you enter the cemetery, the Churchwell graves are near the entrance, just on the left before the Albers monument. George's daughter Rebecca and her husband Charles Wellington Charlton lay beside the Colonel and "Aunt Moody," and just to the west lies a remarkable monument to George's son, Congressman William Montgomery Churchwell and his wife, Martha. Just to the west lie many of George's daughter Laura Churchwell Mabry's family, including many of the Hazens.

Hon. Wm. M. Churchwell,
Departed this life
Aug. 8, 1862
In the full maturity
of manhood. He was a
brave Confederate soldier
who died for the cause
he espoused. He was
distinguished in the
halls of Congress at the
youthful age of 25 for his
brilliant talents and his
eloquence.

*Wm. M. Churchwell tombstone,
Old Gray Cemetery*

William M. Churchwell: The Emperor of Knoxville

His detractors would call him "Louis Napoleon Churchwell: Emperor of Knoxville," but William Montgomery Churchwell was indeed a wealthy and influential attorney, businessman, banker, and two-term Congressman who was appointed by Confederate President Jefferson Davis to be the Provost Marshal over East Tennessee during the Civil War. He is famous for sending a telegram to then Senator Andrew Johnson's wife in Greenville, Tennessee, ordering her out of Confederate territory and on to Nashville. He did the same to the wife of Parson Brownlow. In 1862, at the age of 36, he died suddenly of typhoid in Knoxville, a year before Union forces re-took Knoxville in November 1863 during the Siege of Knoxville.

When Knoxvillians talk about their Second District seat in the United States Congress, they may think the Duncan family has held the seat forever. Actually, John J. "Jimmy" Duncan Jr. and his father, John Duncan Sr., have only held the seat since 1964, a mere 46 years. Pundits claim Republicans have held the seat since the 1850s, but few even know the name of the last Democrat to hold that seat—that honor falls to Congressman William Montgomery Churchwell. Technically, he represented Tennessee's Third District from 1851-1853, and only the Second District from 1853-1855 following redistricting of the Third. In addition, William Sneed, who followed Churchwell, was not in fact a Republican, but belonged to the American Party, and Horace Maynard, the next man to hold the office, was first a Know Nothing, then a member of the Opposition Party from 1859-1861, a member of the Unionist Party from 1861-1863, a member of the Unconditional Unionist Party from 1866-1867, and finally a Republican from 1867-1873.

William Montgomery Churchwell would be very important to Knoxville during the Confederate occupation of the city, and while today he may have slipped into the edges of Knoxville history, Congressman Churchwell was indeed an important figure in Knoxville history. As a Congressman, Churchwell was by any measure a conservative Democrat who fought hard for the preservation of the Union in the decade before the Civil War.

Churchwell, the son of Colonel George Wellington Churchwell and Rebecca Evelyn Montgomery Churchwell, was born "near Knoxville" February 20, 1826, to one of the wealthiest families in the area. His father had begun purchasing lands north of Knoxville along Second Creek—in present-day Oakwood-Lincoln Park—when William was only 2 years old, according to deed records, and the young man would grow up on the family plantation known as Springdale.

Churchwell owes much of his prominence in Knoxville to his father's fortunes, as well as a formal education. In 1840, at the age of 14, he enrolled in the Preparatory and Scientific Department of the East Tennessee University, today the University of Tennessee. The purpose of this department was to prepare young men for enrollment in regular classes. The principal of the department was Horace Maynard, whom Churchwell would defeat in his race for the U.S. Congress only 13 years later.

While enrolled, Churchwell studied Greek, Latin, reading, orthography, penmanship, mental and written arithmetic, geography, history, grammar, single and double-entry bookkeeping, practical surveying and leveling, composition, and linear drawing. A year later, he enrolled as a student in the University Department of East Tennessee University—a non-classical course of study that replaced the Preparatory Department. From 1842-1843, he was a student at Emory and Henry College in Virginia. There, he studied more Latin and Greek, including Horace, Cicero, Socrates, and Plato, as well as Algebra, Geometry, Trigonometry, surveying and navigation, English, rhetoric, composition, and elocution. Uninterested in continuing his college studies past his sophomore year, Churchwell studied law like his father, and got his legal license in 1848.

Around this time, Churchwell married Martha Eleanor Deery, a daughter of the wealthy Deery family of Sullivan County, although the marriage and court records of Sullivan County were burned during the Civil War. He quickly entered into business with his wife's family, J.A. Deery, W.E. Deery, and E. E. Deery, in Deerys & Churchwell Grocery Commission and Forwarding Merchants, and early Knoxville "jobbing" (wholesale) business on Gay Street.

By 1848, he was also the owner of a steamboat company, the Regular Weekly Knoxville and New Orleans Packet Line. This company operated at least four paddlewheelers, including the *Huntsville*, the *Knoxville*, the *Mohican*, and the *George Nicholson*. He also owned the Churchwell Lumber Mills at the mouth of First Creek. Formerly known as Kings Mills, these mills were equipped with their own railroad to haul logs into the river. By 1850, at the young age of 24, Churchwell had property, including slaves, valued at $42,000. In the same year, his father, George Wellington Churchwell, had assets worth only slightly more, at $56,000.

In 1954, Ruth Osborne Turner wrote her Master's Thesis, *The Public Career of William Montgomery Churchwell*, at the University of Tennessee. She went on to teach at Carson Newman College for 31 years. Her thesis includes a detailed account from numerous sources on Churchwell and his two terms in Congress.

In 1851, at age 25, Churchwell began his foray into politics, according to Turner's thesis. He was recruited by the Democratic Party to run for the Third District Congressional seat against the incumbent Josiah McNair Anderson, a Whig from Bledsoe County. A key issue in the campaign was the Compromise of 1850, a complicated series of five legislative bills that quieted secessionist talk for nearly four years, which Churchwell favored, making him distinctively conservative when compared to other Democrats across the state of Tennessee. The Compromise was meant to hold the Union together while dealing with the spread of slavery to western territories. The Whig Party had previously pledged to support the Compromise in their effort to keep the Union from splitting.

The political tools used often Congressman William M. Churchwell are parallel to today, from his method of mud-slinging politics using his opponent's own published words to how he used "pork-barrel spending" to bring much needed improvements to his district.

Churchwell fared well in such a strong Whig district, including many in Knox County who supported him—they felt a conservative Democrat from Knoxville was preferable to one of their own from Bledsoe County, especially on Churchwell's platform, which promised much needed "internal improvements" in roads, railroads, and river navigation.

Churchwell went to Congress that year, and voted for one resolution on the Compromise bill before returning to Knoxville because his wife, Martha, was ill. He was criticized for missing other key votes, and turned to the press to clear himself. The following appeared in the April 13, 1852 *Daily Union* in Washington:

Knoxville, Tennessee
April 13, 1852

Gentlemen: From the papers I see that the Compromise resolutions introduced by the Hon. Mr. Jackson of Georgia, with Mr. Hillyer's amendment, passed the House of Representatives on the 5th instant. I regret my absence from the House at the time the vote was taken, caused by the ill health of my family. Had I been present, I should have voted for the resolution and amendment. The former is similar to Mr. Fitch's resolution, for which I voted. I desire to be recorded in favor of the finality of the Compromise, opposed to every effort that may be made to disturb it, and against all further agitation of the troublesome question.

Very respectfully,
W. M. Churchwell

During Churchwell's first term in Congress, he also supported the very important Homestead Bill, which offered applicants, including freed slaves, up to 160 acres of undeveloped federal land outside of the original 13 colonies. The bill would not pass for another 10 years. Three times—in 1852, 1854, and 1859—the House of Representatives passed homestead legislation, but on each occasion, the Senate defeated it. In 1860, a homestead bill providing Federal land grants to western settlers was passed by Congress only to be vetoed by President Buchanan. It was finally passed and signed by Abraham Lincoln in 1862.

Churchwell represented Knoxville well with what today is known as pork, bringing vital funding for the navigation of the Tennessee river when a pork-barrel bill for river and harbor improvements was being debated.

In 1853, following re-districting, Churchwell was the incumbent candidate for the Second Congressional District instead of the Third. His opponent was Horace Maynard, his old professor from The East Tennessee University, known today as the University of Tennessee. Maynard had spent ten years practicing law and was an eloquent speaker. The campaign that followed was full of mud-slinging, and Churchwell defeated Maynard primarily by bringing forth old columns that Maynard had written for the *Knoxville Times* back in 1839 under the psuedonym Zadock Jones. These Zadock Jones articles, written almost 14 years earlier, were fairly elitist, referring to the masses as the "common hord."

> *"...I again State Distinctly That I Esteem the Herd of Mankind, the human cattle, no better than other cattle, nor quite so good. I hold them in the utmost loathing and contempt," Maynard wrote in one of his essays. In another, he compared equality to moonshine. "Say what you will about natural equality, it is all moonshine, a thing well enough for school boys and theorists to speculate upon and for DEMAGOGUES TO TICKLE THE EARS OF THE RABBLE WITH, BUT A THING WITH FOUNDATION IN FACT, OR PHILOSOPHY AND WHICH IF IT COULD BE CARRIED INTO PRACTICE WOULD BE THE SUBVERSION OF ORDER AND BRING THE MOST DIREFUL CONSEQUENCE UPON INDIVIDUALS AND SOCIETY. Some are as certainly born to rule as others to cultivate music, poetry, or mathematics."*
> *— Horace Maynard, writing as Zadock Jones*

While Maynard pled the statute of limitations on the use of his columns, Churchwell pushed more populist rhetoric against the "monarchical tinge" of Maynard, despite Maynard's own impoverished beginnings, and beat him badly in the election. Ironically, Maynard supporters charged, truthfully, that it was Churchwell who was the friend of the wealthy, having been raised in "a country villa with hosts of servants," a reference to his father's Springdale plantation in present-day Oakwood-Lincoln Park.

Churchwell's supporters argued that Maynard lived in one the fanciest mansions in town, and that Churchwell's father, Colonel George Churchwell, had worked for 25 cents a day in a brickyard and that the doors of the Churchwell home, two miles from town, were open to all, rich or poor. Could that brickyard have been at Arlington, at Broadway and present-day Walker Boulevard? A brickyard is visible on the 1895 map of Knoxville at Arlington (page 76). Nonetheless, the Churchwell home, by all accounts, was indeed quite fine. Following Churchwell's victory over Maynard, Parson Brownlow himself, declared in the *Knoxville Whig*, (it was not yet the "Rebel Ventilator) "We shall not be surprised if in less than five years, he (Churchwell) is Governor of Tennessee. The signs are all that way."

During Churchwell's second term in Congress, a little known amendment to the Warehouse Bill which Churchwell succeeded in making into law would prove to be a major factor in the railroad boom that Knoxville would see by the late 1850s. Churchwell's amendment was for the passage of a credit for railroad companies to pay the duty on iron shipped to them for railroad improvements. Churchwell knew that this would indeed benefit East Tennessee railroads, allowing Knoxville wholesale houses to import directly from cities like Liverpool. This important amendment allowed Knoxville to receive direct shipments from foreign countries instead of from the port cities of the eastern United States.

> **"Few are our days between the cradle and the grave. All things are subject to end and decay. Man, like all else, falls to the earth—to sprout trees and flowers again."**—*William Montgomery Churchwell.*

During his second term in Congress, Churchwell gave one of his longest speeches ever, over the Kansas Nebraska bill, on May 19, 1854. He saw rising opposition from other Tennessee representatives, and became outspoken over the principle that every state was "free and independent." A fight nearly broke out in Congress among the Tennessee delegation. Churchwell was accused of drawing a pistol, which he denied. Other than his accuser, William Cullom of Carthage, Tennessee, no other House members admitted to seeing the pistol.

Although, colorful, eloquent, and effective, Churchwell declined a third term in Congress. He announced his retirement in order to become president of the Knoxville and Kentucky Railroad, succeeding John Crozier. The *Knoxville Statesman* critiqued his Congressional service by saying, "In our humble judgment he has done more the interests of the District in the same length of time, than any of his illustrious predecessors in the Whig school of politics."

Churchwell's service to the railroads was all about financial gain. He was the principal stockholder of the railroad for which he was now president, and he also owned stock in the East Tennessee and Virginia Railroad. The Knoxville and Kentucky line was intended to link Cincinatti and Charleston, and meandered through major coal deposits of the Appalachian Mountains. It would also connect the East Tennessee and Virginia line to the East Tennessee and Georgia line. While president for only two years, Churchwell was successful in helping organize the company, although completion of construction of the line was still some years away. Around the same time, Churchwell also became president of the Bank of East Tennessee in November, 1854. The other officers were A. A. Barnes, William Swan Sr., J. G. M. Ramsey, Campbell Wallace, Charles McGuire, and Churchwell's brother-in-law, Joseph A. Mabry. The bank, chartered in 1843 with capital stock of $800,000, was not in a good financial position when Churchwell became president, and matters quickly got worse. Contributing to the financial condition was the desire of Nashville banks to prevent the presence of an independent bank in East Tennessee. Charges followed that the bank's charter was being passed from speculator to speculator, with five presidents in four years, including Churchwell in 1854. A run on the bank in 1852 had left matters uncertain. Churchwell was also accused of borrowing heavily from his own bank, although he countered that such indebtedness preceeded his tenure as president. Churchwell put up all of his personal real estate, valued at $125,000, to stabilize the bank. The two bank trustees responsible for settling the debts of the bank, Thomas Lyon and J. G. M. Ramsey, were slow in paying off bank creditors, and were accused of showed preferential treatment in selectively paying off certain bank creditors. However, by 1860, many lawsuits were brought against the bank, and Churchwell's reputation was tarnished. The *Knoxville Whig*, formerly a big supporter of Churchwell, now labeled him a "swindler."

During the busy period of the late 1850s when Churchwell was president of the Knoxville and Kentucky Railroad and the Bank of East Tennessee, the former Congressman also found time to continue to dabble in politics, supporting the campaign of James Buchanan for president. Buchanan rewarded his ardent supporter with a special assignment: duty in 1859 as a diplomatic agent to Mexico. It was a time of strained relations between the United States and Mexico. Churchwell was sent to Mexico to gather information on the Juarez government and describe the state of the political parties there, and also to report on the state of the natural resources of Mexico. Finding out what these various political parties in Mexico wanted and expected from the United States laid the groundwork for negotiations on lower California, navigation of the Rio Grande, and reciprocity in trade between the two countries.

Churchwell was briefly considered as a running mate for Stephen Douglas in the 1860 election against Abraham Lincoln, but such discussions faded as the Democratic Party of 1859 became more divided. Churchwell himself thought that only three men, Benjamin Fitzpatrick of Alabama, Francis Pickens of South Carolina, or John Breckinridge of Kentucky could unite the party. Their collective hope was that the nomination of a southerner might indeed prevent the fracturing of the Union.

Following the election of 1860, East Tennessee quickly split between North and South. Recruiting stations at opposite ends of Gay Street opened for the Union and for the Confederacy. Churchwell himself joined the Confederacy in May, 1861. Churchwell assembled a regiment of men from Knox County, and trained them at Camp Sneed, near Knoxville. It was designated the 34th Regiment of Tennessee Infantry, and was also known as the 4th Confederate Regiment of Tennessee Infantry. Churchwell was appointed a Confederate Colonel on August 16, 1861. Under General Felix Zollicoffer, a former Whig Congressman, Churchwell's regiment was dispatched to Cumberland Gap. By October, Churchwell's men were placing cannon at Cumberland Gap, preparing for battle. Zollicoffer ordered Churchwell to further fortify the Gap, with heavy guns, forts, and breastworks. Battling cold weather, lack of supplies and munitions, the 2021 Confederate troops at the Gap, with 836 under Churchwell's command, were less than satisfied with the action, and eagerly wanted to fight. General Zollicoffer was killed at Mill Spring, near Cumberland Gap, January 20, 1862. By February, Churchwell was transferred—back to Knoxville, where Confederate President Jefferson Davis would appoint him Provost Marshal over East Tennessee, under Confederate martial law.

Churchwell was seen as fairly moderate in dealing with Union supporters in East Tennessee. He guaranteed clemency for those wanting to return to their homes after the Confederate occupation of the region, assuming they would lay down their arms and pledge an oath of loyalty to the Confederate States. Churchwell committed himself to the protection of lives and property of the citizens of East Tennessee. Parson Brownlow, in a speech in Cincinatti, claimed that his wife and children were being held hostage in Knoxville by the Confederates—in essence, held hostage by Churchwell. Confederate General Kirby Smith insisted that Churchwell communicate with Mrs. Brownlow that she was indeed free to leave the area. The following letters were published in 1862 by William Gannaway Brownlow (Parson Brownlow) in the book *Sketches of the Rise, Progress, and Decline of Secession: with a Narrative of Personal Adventures Among the Rebels*:

Mrs. W. G. Brownlow, Knoxville:—

Madam :—By Major-General E. Kirby Smith I am directed most respectfully to inform you that you and your children are not held as hostages for the good behavior of your husband, as represented by him in a speech at Cincinnati recently, and that yourself and family will be required to pass beyond the Confederate States line in thirty-six hours from this date. Passports will be granted you from this office. Very respectfully,

W. M. Churchwell, "Colonel and Provost-Marshal."
Knoxville, Tens., April 21,1862.

Colonel W. M. Churchwell, Provost-Marshal:—

Sir :—Your official note as Provost-Marshal for East Tennessee, ordering myself and family to remove beyond the limits of the Confederate States within the next thirty-six hours, is just received; and I hasten to reply to it. My husband, as you are aware, is not here to afford me his protection and counsel; and, being wellnigh in the evening of life, with a family of dependent children, I have to request, as a matter of indulgence, that you extend the time for my exile a few days longer, as to leave within the time prescribed by your mandate would result in the total sacrifice of my private interests. I have to request the further information what guarantee of safety your passport will afford myself and family. Yours, &c,

Eliza A. Brownlow."

Mrs. W. G. Brownlow:—

Madam :—At your request, the time for your leaving to join your husband is extended until Thursday morning next. The route will be via Kingston and Sparta. Your safety will be the soldiers sent along for your protection to the enemy's line.

Very respectfully,
W. M. Churchwell, "Colonel and Provost-Marshal."

Head-quarters, Department East Tennessee, I Office Provost-marshal, Knoxville, April 25, 1862.

The following-named persons are allowed (in charge of Lieutenant Joseph H. Speed) to pass out of the Confederate States Government by way of Norfolk, Va.:— Mrs. Eliza Brownlow and three children. Miss Mary Brownlow. Mrs. Sue C. Sawyers and child. John B. Brownlow.

W. M. Churchwell, "Colonel and Provost-Marshal."

That April, Churchwell similarly demanded that Mrs. Andrew Johnson, the wife of the senator and future president, leave Confederate territory. By May 19, she still had not left, citing her ill health. Churchwell dispatched a deputy marshal to visit her, and he reported back that she was indeed very ill, but her son promised that she would soon leave.

However, in a speech in Nashville, Senator Johnson made a harsh accusation that described the event very differently: "The Confederates went to my home while my wife was sick, my child, eight years old, consumed with consumption. They turned her and the child into the streets, converted my house, built with my own hands into a hospital and barracks. My servants they confiscated. It was with much suffering my wife and little boy were able to reach the home of a relative, many miles away."

Despite the obligations of Provost Marshal Churchwell to safely transport the families of Union women to Federal territory, including the family of Horace Maynard, the environment was obviously politically charged, with many of the accusations of cruelty and malicious intent coming from none other than Parson Brownlow himself. Churchwell, however, ran the office efficiently, with 17 deputy provost marshals serving him. He insisted they make no arrests unless it was absolutely "urgent necessity," and that they use their power with kindness but firmness.

After only a year in the Confederate Army, and after having served the United States as both a Congressman and a foreign diplomat, William Montgomery Churchwell died suddenly from typhoid on August 8, 1862, at only 36 years of age, a full year before Union forces would gather to re-take Knoxville from the Confederacy. He likely was exposed to typhoid during his encampment at Cumberland Gap. While often overlooked in the annals of Tennesee history, Churchwell's contributions during the difficult, contradictory years leading up to the Civil War are worthy of further study, and it is with deep appreciation to Ruth Osborne Turner for the valuable research available from her 1954 Master's thesis.

Early Scott Cabin on First Creek. A photograph from the journal of Edith Scott, granddaughter of Colonel James Scott Jr, depicting an early Scott Cabin on First Creek. *Photo courtesy Edith Scott Collection, McClung Historical Collection.*

The Scotts: Early Settlers

Captain James Scott, Sr. was one of the earliest settlers in the area that would become Oakwood and Lincoln Park, and he was General John Sevier's right-hand man.

James Scott, Sr., a early settler of Blount County, was born in 1760. There is dispute over his place of birth, whether in Ireland or Virginia. He did marry his wife, Jane Adams, in Virginia, and was one of the original signers of the Petition of the Inhabitants of the Western Country presented to the North Carolina legislature in 1787, which called for a separate state for the people living west of the Unaka Mountains, according to the book, *DeArmond Families in America.*

Scott was a soldier in the Indian wars during the 1790s, commanded a regiment and was wounded in battle on the Little Tennessee River. By an act of the Territorial Assembly passed in 1795, a group of territorial justices met at the home of Abraham Wear (of Wear's Valley) to establish Blount County. Those justices included James Scott, as well as William Wallace, William Lowry, Oliver Alexander, David Craig, and George Ewing. A year later, "Captain" Scott was commissioned in the Tennessee Militia, October, 1796.

From the *DeArmond* book:

> *"His first years in Blount County were spent in a blockhouse after which he built a log cabin on his farm which consisted of 640 acres. On at least one occasion after he had built his cabin, he and his wife were forced to return to the blockhouse because of an Indian raid, and James (Scott) with the other men fired through the portholes while his wife and the other women moulded bullets at the hearth. John Sevier called James Scott his "right-hand man" and said he never wanted to go on an Indian campaign without him riding by his side. He was a remarkable woodsman and accompanied Sevier constantly on his forays against the Indians. James Scott served as direct representative from Blount County to the Second General Assembly of the newly formed State of Tennessee, at Knoxville in 1797; in the Third General Assembly in 1799; the Fifth Assembly in 1803; the Sixth Assembly in 1805; and the Seventh Assembly in 1807."*

According to JGM Ramsey's 1853 book, *The Annals of Tennessee*, Colonel Scott would command troops in Sevier's absence on the frontier of Blount County, including forts at Henry's Station, Craig's Station, Ish's Station, and at the block house at Tellico. Each fort was designed with considerable size with a "projection on each square, furnished with port-holes, and calculated to stand a siege by an enemy provided with small arms only."

Despite such early prominence and distinguished service in Blount County, Scott sold his farm and moved to Knoxville sometime after 1815. He first built a log house on North Broadway near what is today Lawson Avenue, directly across Broadway from what would later be his son's flour mill. The house was later covered with clapboard siding, or weatherboard. James Scott Sr. later built a "small brick house" on the west side of First Creek, west of Broadway. He died, without a will, in 1823, and is buried in the cemetery of First Presbyterian Church in downtown Knoxville. Jane, whose sister married Captain Samuel Henley, died in 1837, and is buried next to her husband.

Cedar Grove. Built by Colonel James Scott Jr. in 1833, today, this plantation home is the Stevens Mortuary at Oglewood Avenue and Broadway. *Photo courtesy Thompson Photograph Collection, McClung Historical Collection.*

Cedar Grove: The Scott Plantation

Colonel James Scott, Jr. was a selfless individual who sacrificed himself for his neighbors and friends during Knoxville's 1838 cholera epidemic. By 1833, around the same time Colonel George Churchwell was buying up tracts along Second Creek to the west, there was another plantation house under construction in the same neck of the woods. In fact, the same year Laura Churchwell was born over at Springdale Farm, Colonel James Scott Jr., the son of James Scott Sr. and Jane Adams Scott, built his Cedar Grove farm, also described in historical accounts as being "two miles from Knoxville." It still stands. The Scott house today is known as the Scott-Ledgerwood-Ogle house, so-named for the families who would own it before Tom and Bernice Stevens would buy it in 1958 and open Stevens Mortuary.

Colonel Scott was born on his father's farm in Blount County on March 12, 1797. Moving with his family to Knoxville as a young man, he established the Scott Flour Mills on First Creek, in operation for over 100 years. The mill was located between north Broadway and First Creek, near Coker Avenue.

Aftrer Colonel Scott married Eliza Jane Naomi Bane Alexander Ramsey, the sister of noted historian Dr. J.G.M. Ramsey, and the daughter of Colonel Francis Alexander Ramsey and Peggy Alexander, the couple moved into the little brick house on the west side of Broadway that his father had built. According to the DeArmond account, the little brick house was "across the road" from the new home Scott built for himself with bricks made on-site by his slaves—possibly on the north side of Oglewood today. He then tore down the little brick house.

Unfortunately, Colonel Scott would only enjoy his new home for five short years. He died suddenly, and tragically, during the cholera epidemic that Knoxville endured in 1838. According to William Rule's *Standard History of Knoxville Tennessee*, it would ironically be due to the decomposing matter in the mill ponds along First Creek, including Scott's own millpond, combined with a hot, dry summer, that caused outbreaks of cholera and malaria and drove many Knoxvillians out of the city. For another 45 years, ownership of the home and the farm known as Cedar Grove remains murky, based on county land records. Perhaps his son, Francis Alexander Ramsey Scott, owned it for some time, but FAR Scott is known to have built for himself another great mansion, called Oak Hill, on Oak Hill. This home stood where Saint Mary's Hospital is today.

While according to the Poe map of 1863, "Mrs. Scott" owned the place in that year, it was clearly a series of Scott descendants who must have owned it, as Eliza Scott died in 1837. The ownership of the place after the death of James and Eliza Scott remains uncertain, as one son in ill health moved back to Blount County while FAR Scott continued to operate the mill while building his own mansion on what is today Saint Mary's Hill. But the murky ownership of the home ends when the Honorable Washington Lafayette Ledgerwood bought the house in 1883, 45 years after the death of Colonel James Scott, Jr.

Scott Flour Mills. A team of horses leads a wagon of the Scott Mill Co. In the background is the home of Francis Alexander Ramsey Scott, son of Colonel James Scott Jr. The home was located where St. Mary's Hospital is today. *Photo courtesy Edith Collection, McClung Historical Collection.*

The Scott Flour Mill. The Scott Flour Mill was located on First Creek near Oglewood Avenue. *Photo courtesy Edith Scott Collection, McClung Historical Collection.*

The Scott Flour Mill. Two employees of the Scott Mill Co. prepare to load a wagon at this warehouse. Note homes faintly visible in the left background of the image. *Photo courtesy Edith Scott Collection, McClung Historical Collection.*

The Red Fox:
Speaker Ledgerwood

Captain Washington Lafayette Ledgerwood was the second owner of Cedar Grove from 1883-1911 and served as Speaker of the House of Representatives for the 43rd Tennessee General Assembly.

Ledgerwood was born in Knox County, Tennessee on June 4, 1843, and grew up working on the farm of his father Samuel Ledgerwood, born in Knox County in 1808. He sported a shocking mop of red hair, earning him the moniker later in life, "The Red Fox," both for his appearance as well as his distinguished military service.

His mother, Scena N. Rutherford, was the daughter of Knox County resident Absalom Rutherford, a veteran of the Revolutionary War from Virginia. He was educated in rural schools in Knox County, and was raised by his parents under strict Baptist influence. He was for many years an influential resident of Oakwood, having purchased the residence of Mrs. James Scott, Jr, the widow of Colonel James Scott, in 1883.

In August, 1861, Ledgerwood enlisted in the Union Army down on Gay Street in Knoxville. He served as a private in Company B, First Tennessee infantry, commanded by R. K. Byrd. In April, 1862, he transferred to the Third Tennessee infantry as a first lieutenant of Company I. In May, 1863, he became captain of the company until the end of the war, and served with distinction in Tennessee, Kentucky, Ohio, Alabama, as well as the Georgia campaign.

Staircase at Cedar Grove. The original staircase at Cedar Grove with carpet runner, the home built by Colonel James Scott Jr. in 1833. *Photo courtesy Thompson Photograph Collection, McClung Historical Collection.*

After he mustered out of service in May, 1865 in Nashville, he returned to farming in Knox County. In 1866, he married Jo Strother of Sumner County, Tennessee, in Louisville, Kentucky. Her father, Henry, was a merchant in Gallatin, Tennessee. According to the 1888 book, *Sketches of Prominent Tennesseans* by William Speer, Mrs. Ledgerwood was "educated at Louisville, and is a woman of quiet, domestic habits, and though not unsocial, is essentially a home-maker and a home-lover. She is noted for her frankness, and for her generosity, especially to those in distress."

The same year as his marriage, the Knox County Democratic Party nominated Ledgerwood to the state legislature, but he lost to Dr. M.L. Mynatt. A year later, President Andrew Johnson appointed him second lieutenant in the Eighteenth regular infantry, United States Army.

Much of his service during this period was spent in Arizona and Nebraska, guarding the construction crews of the Union Pacific Railroad. He continued his service in the Army until 1872, when he again returned to Knox County to resume farming.

One anecdote offers a clue to his personality and loyalty. During the impeachment of President Johnson, a fellow officer spoke perjoratively about the President. Lieutenant Ledgerwood beat the officer up, knocked him down, and resigned from the Army, returning to his beloved Knoxville.

While farming, he studied law, and was admitted to the bar in 1873 by Judge E. T. Hall and Chancellor O. P. Temple. He practiced law in Knoxville until 1884, when he purchased Cedar Grove farm from the Scott family.

In 1874, Captain Ledgerwood was again nominated by the Democratic Party to represent Knox County in the state legislature. He won election over Senator S. T. Logan, and served in the 38th General Assembly and chaired the House committee on military affairs. In 1876, he served as a pallbearer at President Andrew Johnson's funeral.

In 1880, he served as elector for the Second Congressional district, and in 1882, was again elected to the state legislature, and was named Speaker of the House of the 43rd General Assembly of the State of Tennessee.

Four years later, he ran against the political machine of Leonidas C. Houk for the U.S. Congress in the Second District, losing narrowly.

Captain Ledgerwood and his wife, Jo, had four children: Claude, born August 16, 1867; Sidney Ailine, born March 15, 1869 at Sidney, on the Union Pacific railroad in what was then the Wyoming Territory (now Nebraska); Samuel T. (Tobe), born September 30, 1870 in Knox County; and Willie, born June 4, 1872, in Knox County.

According to the book, *Sketches of Prominent Tennesseans*, Captain Ledgerwood was noted for his thrift and hard work.

"The only money Capt. Ledgerwood ever had given to him was five hundred dollars, presented by his father after his marriage. All else that he has handled he has made himself by close application to business, by hard work, and by practicing strict economy. Although very cautious about endorsing, he has lost some by security debts. He never sued a client or anybody else in his life on his own account, and has never been sued by any man. A close collector of fees, by making his clients believe he thinks them honest they make unusual exertions to pay him. His standing as a lawyer and a politician comes of his having been always a true man, never lying to or deceiving any one, and fulfilling all promises he makes. He is a man of strong likes and dislikes. His tone of voice indicates a man of decision of character and great self-reliance."

Captain Ledgerwood died in his beloved home in 1911. Eight years later, Dr. Pinkney Nelson Ogle and his wife, Mrs. Edith Henson Ogle, acquired the property from Ledgerwood's son, Tobe Ledgerwood, who had moved to the Halls community.

Edith Henson Ogle. 1890s photograph of Edith Henson Ogle. She and her husband P. N. Ogle carefully restored and expanded Cedar Grove in the 1920s and 1930s, adding plumbing and electricity to the antebellum home. *Photo courtesy Knox County Two Centuries Photograph Project, McClung Historical Collection.*

The Ogles

Pinkney Nelson Ogle and Edith Lenora Henson Ogle owned Cedar Grove from 1919 to 1947. Dr. Ogle was a well-respected Knoxville dentist who was born in Sevier County in 1878, the son of Eli Ogle and Sarah McMahan. He regularly contributed to national medical journals. In a 1917 edition of the monthly *Dental Summary*, he writes "…There is one point I want to speak of, and that is with regard to the impression we leave with our patients. We cannot lay down any concrete rule to go by. When a stranger comes to us, one who may never have heard of us, he comes in and gets his first impression and that impression is going to be a lasting one, and you must make it a good one. And you treat one fellow one way and perhaps you have won his friendship, whereas you treat another fellow the same way, and perhaps you have made him an enemy. And so you have to read human nature, and treat every man in such a way as in your judgment will gain his confidence."

Dr. Ogle's wife, Edith, was apparently more than a gracious host, she was also his hardworking dental assistant. As early as 1936, she was invited to speak nationally before the American Dental Assistants Association. "We have even invited a WIFE to appear on this program, and Mrs. P. N. Ogle, wife of Dr. Ogle of Knoxville, will give us her views on the Dental Assistant," according to Volume 5 of *The Dental Assistant* magazine, published in 1936.

On November 26, 1934, The Knoxville *News Sentinel* featured an extensive article about the home

Cedar Grove, Hand-Painted Wallpaper. A likely 1940s Thompson photograph of the interior of Cedar Grove, before the famous wallpaper was removed. It now hangs in the dining room of the Armstrong Lockett House, known as Crescent Bend, on Kingston Pike. Crescent Bend is available for tours and special events. *Photo courtesy Thompson Photograph Collection, McClung Historical Collection.*

then owned by Dr.. Pinkney Nelson Ogle and Mrs. Edith Henson Ogle. The article, titled *Old Home Has Charm of Antiquity: Famous Ledgerwood House Features Parisian Wallpaper and Hand-Made Bricks*, was written when the house was 101 years old. A photo of Mrs. Ogle with her arm on the high mantel above the fireplace graces the article, and describes her as the "present mistress of the house."

According to the 1920 U.S. Census, The Ogles lived in the home with Dr. Ogle's two children from his marriage to Sarah Ellen Williams, who died in 1916: Bernard Simeon, age 12, and Ina May age 16, as well as some of Edith's family, including Jesse and Emma Henson, ages 49 and 45, and Bryan and May Smith, ages 25 and 21. Ina May Ogle married Walter Ogg and moved to Los Angeles, California. Bernard died in Knoxville in 1961.

Several key features of the Scott-Ledgerwood-Ogle home are described in this 1934 article, including the scenic wallpaper, "in vivid hues which have faded little in the century since it was hung, presents reproductions of scenes from the Gardens of Versailles."

According to this source, the famous wallpaper may have an intriguing history, both for its acquisition and its installation by an ex-pirate. John Stacks was "one of Lafitte's men who helped Andrew Jackson while the British at New Orleans in the War of 1812," according to one account. Intrigued by the stories of virgin forests from "Jackson's coon-capped riflemen," Stacks followed these Tennesseans back from New Orleans. He arrived in Knoxville and established himself as a painter and wallpaper hanger. He also became Knoxville's first town marshal.

By 1833, when Colonel James Scott, Jr. was building this home, he consulted with Stacks about suitable hand-painted wallpaper. The Colonel, successful with his flour mill, ordered the paper from Paris. It arrived in New Orleans and was transported by flatboat to Knoxville. Another account tells that Andrew Jackson originally ordered the wallpaper, heard that it had burned on the boat, and ordered more, thus allowing Scott to obtain one of the shipments.

Also of note in the home was the simple, handcarved banister with its lacy balustrade which still graces the front hall's open staircase to the left of the fireplace. The walls of the two-story home were made from slave-made brick manufactured on the original Scott farm. The Ogles added electricity and running water to the home in 1919.

Dr. Ogle died February 23, 1947, and his family sold Cedar Grove to Oglewood Baptist Church, pastored by Reverend Frank Clifton, for $35,000 in June, 1947. At the time, the home and the four-acre lot contained many trees which had been planted as a hobby by Colonel Ledgerwood.

Although the church committed to "do as much as possible to preserve the antiquity of the home," the decision was made to remove the wallpaper from the home in order to preserve it. By 1951, the church donated the wallpaper to the University of Tennessee's Frank McClung Museum, which supervised its removal along with Nancy McClelland, a leading expert in antique wallpapers and Mrs. Belle Ingram, who lived at 1013 West Fourth Avenue and was an expert in steaming and papering. According to McClelland, the wallpaper pattern was called "Le Petit Décor," and was printed in Paris in 1830 by Joseph Defour.

The wallpaper, on loan to the Toms Memorial Collection, now hangs in the dining room of the Armstrong Lockett House, known as Crescent Bend, on Kingston Pike.

By 1959, Oglewood Baptist Church encountered financial difficulties, and the church was merged into Broadway Baptist Church. The church had no use for Cedar Grove, and it remained vacant and was vandalized for several years, before Thomas and Bernice Stevens purchased the home in 1961 and converted it to Stevens Mortuary.

Oak Hill. The lavish mansion that was Oak Hill, the home of Francis Alexander Ramsey (FAR) Scott. FAR Scott developed several of the neighborhoods around his grand estate, including Scott's Oak Hill addition. *Photo courtesy Mercy Health Partners.*

Saint Mary's Hill

Saint Mary's Hospital has been a major partner in the Oakwood-Lincoln Park community for more than 80 years, both by providing health services and by being a part of the economic and social life of the community as a major employer, along with the jobs provided by independent physicians offices and ancillary health services.

Dedicated on April 22, 1930, the new hospital received its first patient at 10:30 that evening, six-year-old Lillian Howell. Dr. M. J. Reynolds removed her tonsils the next morning.

The need for the hospital was evident as early as 1919, when only about 220 beds were available between the old Knoxville General Hospital, which opened in 1902 with 200 beds over on North Central Street, and the Howard Henson Hospital on Kingston Pike, which only offered 20 beds and was little more than a clinic. These existing facilities were inadequate to meet the burden of hundreds of soldiers returning from World War I with crippling injuries and infections that required long-term medical attention.

Daniel DeWine, a local businessman, had for quite some time been concerned about the health of his daughter, Mamie, and wanted a good Catholic hospital built in Knoxville. It was difficult at the time to take Mamie across the mountains to Asheville, North Carolina for treatment.

Dan Dewine. Dan Dewine, who lived on Armstrong Avenue in Old North Knoxville, donated the seven acres on which St. Mary's Hospital was built. Dewine, born near Third Creek in 1865, had been a policeman, as well as a partner with the sons of Patrick Sullivan. Around 1900, Patrick Sullivan's Saloon became known as Dewine and Sullivan's. *Photo courtesy Mercy Health.*

DeWine bought the old landmark home of Francis Alexander Ramsey Scott, a deserted Victorian home on Oak Hill in what had been the City of Oakwood until 1917, when it was annexed by the City of Knoxville. "It was one of the best looking pieces of property in North Knoxville, an estate of more than seven acres," DeWine said.

DeWine offered the property to the Catholic Church through Rev. Alphonse J. Smith, Bishop of Tennessee, for a "Sisters hospital in memory of his deceased daughter, Mamie."

Bishop Smith offered the land to the Sisters of Mercy but "made it clear that no further financial aid could be provided from the church."

In the summer of 1927, two nuns, Sister Mary Pauline Gray and Sister Mary Thomas Dauner were sent from Nashville to begin fundraising for the new hospital, which Bishop Smith had named St Mary's in honor of the Virgin Mary and Mamie DeWine. One of their first calls was to Mrs. Guy (Blanche Allison) Darst, wife of Guy Darst, a rising coal company executive, who was himself an ardent Methodist helping raise funds for the construction of the new Church Street United Methodist Church.

Assisted by Mrs. Darst, the Sisters met with Knoxville doctors to gauge their level of support. Today, the altar at which Mrs. Darst and these sisters prayed for the financial gifts necessary to construct this hospital still stands in the lobby of the original part of the hospital, and stands as a testament to the commitment and vision of these women.

After visiting over 30 medical facilities, the Sisters returned, ready to publicly announce their commitment.

According to the book, *A Calling That Continues*, the commemorative history of St. Mary's Health System at 75 years, "At the request of Sister Mary Pauline, Dr. Kyle C. Copenhaver, President of the Knoxville Medical Society, called a special meeting at 1 p.m. on September 13, 1921, at which time some sixty doctors pledged "our moral support and also our financial support insofar as we feel able to do it for the successful promotion and establishment of this hospital."

"By July, $313,727 had been pledged, more than the goal of $300,000. The new St. Mary's Hospital was on its way," according to the book.

St. Mary's Hospital. Completed in 1930, St. Mary's Hospital continues to be a major contributor to the Oakwood-Lincoln Park community. *Photo courtesy Mercy Health.*

Dogwoods in Bloom. Dogwoods and tulips are in full bloom at Cedar Grove, the Scott-Ledgerwood-Ogle House that is today the home of Stevens Mortuary, begun by Tom and Bernice Stevens in 1958. *Photo courtesy Bernice Stevens.*

Stevens Mortuary

As you drive north on Broadway, the little yellow bungalow home at the corner of Broadway and Raleigh Avenue across from Vic and Bill's deli is hard to miss. In recent years, it has been a tattoo parlor and a hot tub repair shop, among other things.

But in 1958, Tom and Bernice Stevens opened Stevens Mortuary in that humble little Lincoln Park home. In 2008, the Stevens family celebrated its 50th anniversary of their business in a much larger home—the building they acquired in 1961—Cedar Grove Plantation at Oglewood Avenue and Broadway. Today, Stevens Mortuary continues to be a family-owned and operated funeral home and is highly respected in the community for serving families in a professional and compassionate way.

Following Tom Stevens' death in 1978, Bernice Stevens committed herself to continuing the vision she and her husband had started twenty years before.

Mrs. Stevens carefully selects her staff, making sure that they share her commitment to help families during the difficult time of losing a loved one–and consider it a privilege to do so. Her sister, Mary E. Cantwell, is a funeral director/ embalmer and oversees the day-to-day business operations.

As visitors turn into the driveway from Oglewood Avenue, they might think they are approaching a beautiful plantation home. Indeed they are approaching the home originally built in 1833 by Col.

Cedar Grove, The Scott-Ledgerwood-Ogle House, as It Appears Today. A restored parlor of Stevens Mortuary, as it appears today. *Photo courtesy Bernice Stevens.*

James Scott, Jr. and his wife, Eliza Jane Ramsey Scott. Situated on five acres bordered by a creek, the setting, while in the middle of a busy, urban area, is surprisingly beautiful and serene. In years past, Stevens Mortuary has hosted an Easter Sunrise Service that is held on the grounds amid spring-flowering trees, bulbs, and plants.

Tom and Bernice Stevens deserve amazing credit for the restoration and survival of the original Cedar Grove home. After the Ogles, the home was purchased by Oglewood Baptist Church, which had plans for converting the home into a church. That effort proved unsuccessful, and after that church merged with Second Baptist Church (now Centerpointe Baptist on Broadway), the building was no longer needed. Sitting vacant during much of the 1940s and 1950s, the Stevens rescued the home from vandals and vagrants, purchasing it and lovingly restoring it in a manner that Edith Henson Ogle would likely approve.

Although the building has been added onto to accomodate the needs of a modern mortuary, both the interior and exterior of the home are clearly recognizable, and the interior is exquisitely decorated with period antiques, including four square-grand pianos.

Forgotten Home on Broadway. This large bungalow home once stood on Broadway near Atlantic Avenue, the home of Mr. and Mrs. Godfrey Scheitlin, Jr. He operated Scheitlin and Clark, music and musical merchandise, at 143 Gay Street as early as 1890. His father, Godfrey Scheitlin, Sr. settled in the Lincoln Park/Arlington area around the the time of the Civil War, and the father's large farm is noted on the 1863 Orlando Poe map (page 16) adjacent to Broadway, although it was known as The Tazewell Pike at the time. *Photo courtesy Knox County Two Centuries Photograph Project, McClung Historical Collection.*

The Scheitlins

Godfrey (Gottfried) Scheitlin Sr. , born in Switzerland in 1821, came to Knoxville in the mid-1800s because of its climatic advantages. He passed away in 1896, his two sons Godfrey Jr. and Albert Scheitlin and his daughter, Mrs. Henry Zollinger of New York City at his side.

Despite a childhood of poor health, the elder Scheitlin began his young adult life as an apprentice to a manufacturer of cotton fabrics, before operating his own mills in Europe, employing hundreds of workers. A war between Austria and Italy in 1847 destroyed much of his business. He sold what he had left, reaching New York in August 1848. Ten days later, he was in West Virginia, following his sister and brother-in-law, Mr. and Mrs. John C. Oswald. There he operated a general merchandise store before going west to Minneapolis, Minnesota, and got involved in the foreign exchange business, including the trading of ginseng and gold. After the Civil War and the collapse of gold prices, he began manufacturing linseed oil and paints.

In 1863, during a trip to New York City, he met and married Miss Sophie Behn, and had three living children, and five more who did not live to adulthood, apparently. Leaving the cold Minnesota winters behind, the family settled on a 20-acre farm located on the east side of North Broadway, extending from Edgewood Avenue northward to First Creek and from Broadway eastward about one thousand feet to a street running parallel to Broadway. The home featured a barn almost as large as the house, and a very large carriage house.

In a July 25, 1949 Knoxville *News Sentinel* column by Miss Lucy Templeton, a cousin, Mrs. Mathilde Scheitlin Deaver describes the Scheitlin farm:

> *"Directly after the Civil War, my grandfather, Godfrey Scheitlin Sr. decided to come south in search of a homestead in a milder climate. He first traveled to Atlanta, and was quite favorably impressed. However on his return north he decided to stop over here and investigate. Colonel Perez Dickinson took them in his carriage out to Island Home, driving down the avenue of trees through which the streetcars later ran. They were shown the Champion property, or farm, on Broadway, which extended from Hal Dick's store (or Hal Dic Corner, at Edgewood Avenue) to First Creek at Chicamauga and back to the Chavannes property on Edgewood. Mrs. Fannie Anderson, (Shannon Anderson's mother) lived there at the time. When I was a small child the creaking of farm wagons could be heard as far as Arlington. The roads were narrow, deep in dust, and bordered with many willows and elderberry bushes. There were no street lights, no streetcars. This was indeed country. Since then, of course, one means of transportation gives way to another, each faster than the last, requiring wider streets. If I am not mistaken, three times property has had to be taken, trees and all, as traffic encroached, and today there remains hardly a vestige of the dear dead days of not too long ago."*

The Scheitlins had beautiful June apple trees, pear trees, chestnut trees and a fine grape vineyard. They were expert wine makers and converted some of the wine into vinegar. There was an unusually large two-story wood frame house on the property with a wide porch across the entire front. The back porch was about twenty five feet square, with a cistern built underneath. Rainwater from the roof was filtered through charcoal and stored in the cistern, with another storage tank located in the attic. From this tank, water flowed by gravity to the kitchen and bathroom. The bathtub was a wooden frame shaped like a bathtub, having copper sheet formed to fit inside the frame. All of the joints were soldered and watertight.

According to *Genealogy of Scheitlin Families, National and International*, by Herbert Ivan Scheitlin, Whittet and Shepperson, 1986, almost all of the Scheitlins neighbors in what would have been the Lincoln Park/Arlington section of north Knoxville had horses and carriages. "Grandfather Scheitlin" also had a surrey with a fringed top. The main driveway entrance to the Scheitlin farm near present-day Fairmont and Emoriland featured a pair of double-swinging gates rigged in such a manner that when a buggy was leaving the yard, a wheel would roll over a linkage, causing the gates to automatically swing open. The wheel of the gate would then roll over a corresponding linkage outside of the gates which caused the gates to automatically swing back to the closed position.

Clay Brown Atkin, 1864-1931, was the developer of the city of Oakwood. Portrait of Clay Brown Atkin in a horse-drawn buggy. The driver is possibly the Sheriff. *Photo courtesy Russell Harrison Collection, McClung Historical Collection.*

C.B. Atkin: Tennessee's Most Successful Businessman

Clay Brown Atkin was a noted Knoxville industrialist born in 1864 during the Civil War. He developed the C.B. Atkin Company near the Knoxville, Cumberland Gap, and Louisville Railroad line at the foot of Sharp's Ridge in the 1880s.

The business was actually founded by his father, S.T. Atkin, in 1874 at the same location where C.B. Atkin would grow the business into a small empire. The original S.T. Atkin factory was very small, with about 25 workers.

At the age of 22, in 1886, C.B. Atkin joined the firm, which was then re-named S.T.

> **Author's Note.**
> This chapter was written by the author's 12-year-old son, Jacob Knox Chandler McDaniel, a sixth-grader at First Lutheran School. This is Jacob McDaniel's first published work.

MANUFACTURERS OF
FINE FURNITURE FOR

LIVING ROOMS
DINING ROOMS
✗BEDROOMS

*Kelley
1958*

Atkin

C. B. ATKIN COMPANY ... KNOXVILLE, TENNESSEE

IN THE RICH
HERITAGE OF
EARLY AMERICA ...

**Ameritage°
Maple**

COLLECTION

in Parchwood Finish

AUTHENTICALLY CRAFTED OF
SOLID HARDROCK MAPLE BY

Atkin

Neighborhood consumers. Paul and Norma Kelley purchased their hardrock maple dining room suite around 1958 directly from the C.B. Atkin Co., and still have the original tags to the furniture. *Photo courtesy Norma and Paul Kelley.*

Atkin and Co. In 1889, C.B.. Atkin became the sole owner, and changed the name of the firm name to the C.B. Atkin Co.

Atkin grew the company quickly. By 1918, the factory was four stories high, covered nearly an entire block, and was well equipped with the newest machinery of the time. Their main product was wardrobes, or chiffarobes, as they were then called, and mantels.

According to *The Furniture Worker* magazine, Volume 35, January, 1918, C.B. Atkin also created several subsidiary companies, including the Oakwood Manufacturing Co., in 1902. The Oakwood Manufacturing Co. produced mantels and furniture, including library tables and buffets. At his North Avenue location in Lincoln Park, he also established The Tennessee Table Co. This factory was four stories high, and measured 50x200 feet. The Oakwood Manufacturing Co. occupied a factory 3 stories high, and measured 52x215 feet, in addition to a three-story warehouse. At its height, the C.B. Atkin Co. ranked among one of the most important mantel and furniture manufacturers in the country, and employed over 450 workmen up until the 1960s.

In addition to these businesses, Mr. Atkin planned the very community in which he would grow these companies. Purchasing the heavily wooded oak forest north of Woodland Avenue from Mrs. Sophia Moody Park Churchwell, he began development of the City of Oakwood in 1902.

In 1906, as Oakwood was successfully growing, he was involved in several other large real estate businesses, including the development of the 80-room Colonial Hotel on Gay Street. In 1910, he erected the 200-room Atkin Hotel, one of the most modern hotels in the South at the time. It was located at the corner of Gay Street and Depot, and is today the parking lot of the Regas Restaurant. He was also involved in renovations to the Lamar House, originally a hotel, successfully converting the building into the Bijou Theater. He also built the ten-story Burwell Building, which he named in honor of his wife, Miss Mary Burwell, a native of Pennsylvania.

Atkin was described at the time as having "that rare quality so necessary to achieve success, in that he has surrounded himself with lieutenants, chief of whom is Mr. H. Van Gilder, general manager of the three factories. He has many employees who have been in his service for over a quarter of a century."

Atkin built for himself a grand home on Main Street in downtown Knoxville. The Atkins also spent summers at their country home, Edelmar, seven miles from the city on the Tennessee River. The name of "Edelmar" was made up from the first syllables of the names of Mr. Atkin's three daughters, in order of their birth Edith, Eleanor, Marion. After Mrs. Atkin died in 1949, the family never returned to Edelmar.

Atkin also engaged in small-scale farming. One nine acre tract he farmed in 1917 produced 600 bushels of corn. When he purchased it in 1913, the land was in very poor condition, but Atkin enjoyed learning about and using modern fertilization methods to make the land productive. He considered farming on this small tract his hobby, practicing intensive farming techniques that were not common at the time.

Ameritage Maple ...BEAUTY FOR THE YEARS

An inspired treatment of Early America's furniture masterpieces, the Ameritage Collection offers the lasting charm, true-grained richness and inner radiance of solid hardrock maple . . . given new character and livability by Atkin's meticulous craftsmen. So traditional in concept . . . so superbly constructed . . . so modestly priced . . . so luxurious in its exclusive Parchwood finish!

1 Durably made for the years, with double-reinforced construction. Center-guided drawers with finished interiors.

2 Tops, ends and fronts of solid hardrock maple; antiqued brass hardware patterned after Colonial originals.

3 Exquisite hand-rubbed Parchwood finish, exclusively yours only on Ameritage.

YESTERDAY'S CHARM . . . TODAY'S VALUE . . . TOMORROW'S HEIRLOOM—BY *Atkin*

C.B. Atkin Company. Into the 1960s, the C.B. Atkin Company specialized in traditional, American heritage furniture styles, and prided itself on quality, craftsmanship, and modest pricing. *Photo courtesy Norma and Paul Kelley.*

Oakwood Sales Office. C.B. Atkin's sales office with a sign that read "Homes for Sale, Easy Terms" was located on the northeast corner of North Central at Springdale Avenue. Atkin's sales literature read, "When you need more information or you have selected your lot, go by the office and speak with Mike Shetterly. You will not be disappointed with Oakwood and the way of life it offers your family." Note the raised wooden sidewalks. *Photo courtesy Russell Harrison Collection, McClung Historical Collection.*

Oakwood: The Magic Suburb

In 1902, a beautiful forest with a country road running through it became a lovely village of 131 homes in just three years. Oakwood, the brain child of Clay Brown Atkin, became home to many families who realized they could afford to purchase rather than rent, enjoyed phenomenal rapid growth. Burwell Street was named for his wife, Mary Burwell Atkin, before they married. It was rambling acreage with natural beauty and vistas.

C.B. Atkin, owner of the C.B. Atkin Mantel Factory was a visionary who in three years transformed a forest into a beautiful community of homes, with churches, macadamized streets, running water, electric and gas utilities and electric cars which ran every fifteen minutes. Mr. Atkin bought the property from Sophia Moody Park Churchwell shortly before her death in 1898, and he made promises to the purchasers of what would be done to the property. It was a speculative development

Oakwood. Panoramic view of Oakwood, looking northward up North Central Street. Note the streetcar at left, Sharp's Ridge in the background. *Photo courtesy Russell Harrison Collection, McClung Historical Collection.*

The Busy Streets of Oakwood. A horse-drawn carriage moves down Caldwell Avenue in this early image of Oakwood. *Photo courtesy Russell Harrison Collection, McClung Historical Collection.*

that promised much in breezy sales literature that described a "magic suburb." A 1905 booklet published by C.B. Atkin makes such a promise in its title, *Oakwood: The Magic Suburb with all City Conveniences!* "This little Booklet shows you how a forest of One hundred and Thirty-One Acres has been developed into a beautiful Suburb of nearly Two hundred Homes, inside of Three Years. Read it carefully. It is a part of Knoxville's history and will interest you."

The Oakwood office was a twelve minute walk to the Southern Railway shops where over 1600 men were employed at very good wages, many of them moving to Oakwood. The residents of Oakwood were not limited to the employees of the railway company. Early records indicate that the owners were conductors, craftsmen, engineers, doctors, lawyers, merchants, machinists, school teachers, ministers and trades people.

Early stores were Dr. A.D. Albright's Drug Store where Dr. H.T. McClain had an office above the drug store, and Stallings Grocery Store. In 1917, the General Assembly by private act added Lonsdale, Park City, Mountain View and Oakwood to the City of Knoxville and Oakwood ceased to be a separate entity.

A planned community, Oakwood benefitted from placement of amenities and improvements before a single lot was sold. Mr. Atkin wanted simple restrictions so property rights were ensured. He declared that Oakwood lots were as safe as Government bonds. One dwelling was permitted per lot. Views were protected with the 25' setbacks. No shacks were allowed. Lot prices varied from $100 to $400 per lot with very easy terms which were appealing to newlyweds. The most expensive lot was $8 cash and $8 per month. No interest was charged and there were no mortgages. Deeds were issued when the first payment was made. If a lot was sold to a man and wife, only the man's name was recorded at the Register of Deeds. Owners received a warranty deed when the final payment was made.

As Mr. Atkin said in his sales brochure, "take the Oakwood car and get off at the Oakwood office on Springdale. Look Oakwood over. Nothing is misrepresented. When you need more information or you have selected your lot, go by the office and speak with Mike Shetterly. You will not be disappointed with Oakwood and the way of life it offers your family."

Morelia Avenue. An early view of Morelia Avenue. Note the streetcar tracks with the cars in the distance, as well as the delivery wagon from a carpet trading company from East Vine Avenue in Knoxville. *Photo courtesy Russell Harrison Collection, McClung Historical Collection.*

Beautiful Woodlands. The rural nature of the original Oakwood development is apparent here in this image from Quincy Avenue. *Photo courtesy Russell Harrison Collection, McClung Historical Collection.*

The Tidy Homes of Burwell Avenue. A tree-lined Burwell Avenue is visible here. Note the picket fences. *Photo courtesy Russell Harrison Collection, McClung Historical Collection.*

Name That Street. This view looks east on Warren Avenue, today known as Oglewood Avenue, perhaps west of present-day Glenwood or Kenyon. *Photo courtesy Russell Harrison Collection, McClung Historical Collection.*

Aerial View of Lincoln Park. McMillan Street at Morelia is visible in the foreground, with C.B. Atkin Co. also visible. Sharp's Ridge is in the background. *Photo courtesy Thompson Photograph Collection, McClung Historical Collection.*

The Town of Lincoln Park

In the late nineteenth century, the Edgewood Land and Improvement Company at 624 ½ South Gay Street in Knoxville began to plat lots for a suburban development in a thickly wood section north of Knoxville called Sharp's Gap. That development would become Lincoln Park. Twelve lots were purchased between 1894-1899. Prices averaged three to five hundred dollars per parcel. Three of these lots had preconstructed homes on them according to the Register of Deeds. A one and a half story cottage could be built for $900. Edgewood targeted the working class and used various incentives to appeal to potential buyers such as no mortgages, interest, or notes. Without using banks, buyers with small incomes had more flexibility for home ownership. Payments were small and life insurance was free. The deed was free if death occurred before the home was paid off. Financing was handled through Edgewood's office. It was thought that the company, by targeting this market, would give the average working class family a chance for home ownership. The Washington Avenue Addition in Park City, by contrast, being developed simultaneously by the Edgewood Land and Improvement Company, was at a higher economic level initially, as the company did not think the Knoxville area could support two affluent communities. The company therefore intentionally chose to market Lincoln Park initially to blue collar workers and laborers, even though both developments ended up with a strong mix of both professional and working class families, just as they do today.

First Home in Lincoln Park? Sam and Annie Gilmer on the front porch of their home at 520 Chicamauga, across the street from the newly constructed Lincoln Park School in this circa 1910 image. The Gilmer home was one of the earliest constructed in Lincoln Park. *Photo courtesy Ruth Ann Rogers and Ann Watson.*

Lincoln Park was architecturally appealing with many of the small cottage-type homes resembling George F. Barber designs strategically placed on two hundred acres in the Northwest sector of Knoxville. Sharp's Ridge, formerly known as McAnnally's Ridge in the 1890s and prior to that as Roseberry Ridge, was the northernmost edge of the community. The lots were steep but offered views of the city and the Smoky Mountains. Broadway was the north south corridor and Central flowed east west. Lincoln Park was designed with sixteen streets. Many of the street names changed when the area was annexed into Knoxville in 1917.

Rail service via the Knoxville, Cumberland Gap and Louisville Railroad, and a steam driven trolley system, originally called the Fountain City Dummy Line, cut through Lincoln Park. In 1905, the steam driven Dummy Line was replaced with more modern electric street cars. The Knoxville, Cumberland Gap and Louisville Railroad provided transportation for goods to be carried from local manufacturing plants. The trolley offered transportation for the residents to go downtown for shopping and visiting.

By 1902, forty seven people resided in Lincoln Park, most of them working in industry. Many of the residents worked for the Southern Railway Company. A major incentive was the feasibility of walking to work. It was a working community. By 1905, the population continued to boom.

Several commercial buildings were built as well as churches and schools. Children attended Lincoln Park School on Chicamauga Avenue. There was a local market for grocery items. Lincoln Park supported several early churches. See the chapter on churches beginning on page 113. Lincoln Park continued to expand and by 1906-1907 the city directory noted one hundred and fifty two residents. Broadway Manufacturing Company on Atlantic Avenue brought building supplies to the area which encouraged growth.

By 1907, white-collar workers began to live and work in Lincoln Park. It was becoming a mixed suburb of white and blue collar workers. It was a stable community with little turnover of home sales. Growth subsided by 1910, but houses continued to be sold. The Edgewater Land Improvement Company ceased active marketing after 1910, but through additional research, we find that Lincoln Park continued as a vital stepping stone to Knoxville's residential and commercial history.

Many local Knoxvillians familiar with the old neighborhoods may know that 1917 was a watershed year in the growth of the city. It was in that year that Knoxville annexed the incorporated cities of Oakwood, Park City, Mountain View, and Lonsdale. Unincluded in most texts, however, is the fact that the town of Lincoln Park was also annexed in that year. In other histories, Lincoln Park is frequently considered a suburb of Knoxville, but not a town.

But thanks to Charles R. Ausmus, the former pastor of Lincoln Park Baptist Church (1947-1974), and to Edith Viles, for sharing this important document with us, we learn that Lincoln Park continued to grow after 1910, actually registering with the state of Tennessee as an incorporated town in 1913. Ausmus wrote a short, but very important history of the town of Lincoln Park and of the Church. Ausmus writes:

In the records of the Senate of the State Legislature, entitled Chapter 102, Senate Bill #179, by Senator Morrell and I quote:

"An act to incorporate the town of Lincoln Park, in Knox County, Tennessee, to define the corporate limits thereof, this Act adopted September 27, 1913 and signed by Governor Ben W. Hooper. The corporate limits of "The Town of Lincoln Park" were as follows: "Start on Broadway at an alley 150 feet north of Hiawassee Avenue, go west to the railroad, north to Fairfax, west along Sharp's Ridge to Metler property, south to railroad; east to Pershing Street; south to Shamrock, west to Broadway, north to point of beginning."

Ausmus continues: "The same session of the Legislature passed a resolution setting up certain Commissioners as the governing body of the town of Lincoln Park. There were five commissioners: 1. Chairman of the Board of Commissioners. 2. Commissioner of Finance. 3. Commissioner of Streets and Police. 4. Commissioner of Education. 5. Commissioner of Public Health."

While its origins date back to the late 1880s, Lincoln Park was late in incorporating, and that incorporation would prove even more short-lived than its surrounding sister cities: Oakwood, Lonsdale, Park City, and Mountain View. After the 1917 annexations, Knoxville would then boast a population of 35,000 people.

LINCOLN PARK SCENE, AND THE EPSOM, LITHIA AND CHALYBEATE MINERAL SPRINGS.

Lincoln Park Postcard. Circa 1904 postcard from Lincoln Park, showing early homes along Atlantic or Chicamauga Avenue (top) and the Lincoln Park Mineral Springs pavilion (below) built around the "epsom, lithia, and chalybeate mineral springs" that made the area so popular. The pavilion was located on the grounds of present-day Lincoln Park School. *From the book* Pictures of Knoxville (Tennessee) 1904 *by Russell Harrison. Photo courtesy Charles Reeves, ReevesMaps.com.*

Industrialization in Oakwood and Lincoln Park. The Coster Shop rail yards, a railroad repair facility, south of Sharp's Gap circa 1950's with Lincoln Park visible in the distance. The Lonsdale area begins west (to the left of) the railroad tracks in this image. *Photo courtesy Johnny McReynolds.*

Ersatz National Bank? It's not a real bank, but students at Lincoln Park School are practicing the principles of accounts receivable and accounts payable with their own "Lincoln Park National Bank." Note their little bank books as they wait their turn to speak with a teller. Is the bank president making loans? *Photo courtesy Thompson Photo Collection, McClung Historical Collection.*

NCOLN PARK

IGA

606 CHICAMAUGA AVENUE
PHONE 523-1006
STORE HOURS — 8 am to 7 pm
(Mon. - Sat.)

ON SUNDAY

FOOD STAMPS REDEEMED

4th of JULY

IGA 20 OZ.
BREAD
FOR **$1.00**

BIG ROLL KLEENEX
TOWELS
39¢

SALE!

9 OZ. I.G.A.
TATO CHIPS
49¢

MRS. KINSERS
SALADS
10¢ OFF REGULAR PRICE ON ANY ITEM

MEDIUM
EGGS
DOZ. **39¢**

26 OZ. I.G.A.
CATSUP
49¢

I.G.A. TABLERITE FRESH
GROUND BEEF
LB. **69¢**

I.G.A. TABLERITE CUBE
STEAK
LB. **$1.39**

LARGE RIPE
ANTALOUPE
EACH **59¢**

TRAY
TOMATOES
39¢

NEW 32 OZ. RETURNABLE 4 FLAVORS
ROOT BEER, ORANGE, DIET RITE
RC COLA
4 FOR **$1.00**

10 LB. BAG
CHARCOAL

JUST-RITE HOTDOG
SAUCE

ROYAL SCOTT
MARGARINE

39-Cent Eggs. Sales flyer for the IGA Store at 606 Chicamauga in Lincoln Park. Out of respect for history, this book uses the traditional spelling, without the "K." *Photo courtesy Thompson Photo Collection, McClung Historical Collection.*

Spaulding Grocery. Grady Spaulding ran a grocery on Chicamauga Avenue, two blocks east of Lincoln Park School. Grady is in the photo at left. The young man on the bicycle is unknown in this circa 1929 image. *Photo courtesy Grady Amman.*

A History of Getting Attention for Needed Improvements. Determined to end "a 30-year drought of municipal improvements in their community, militant Lincoln Park residents organized a civic association last night," the 1950s newspaper clipping reads. Their first objective: better bus service. Officers elected were, left to right: George H. Smiley, vice president, Carl R. Bailes, president, Mrs. A.S. Preston, secretary, and John R. Gilmer, treasurer. *Photo courtesy Ruth Ann Rogers and Ann Watson.*

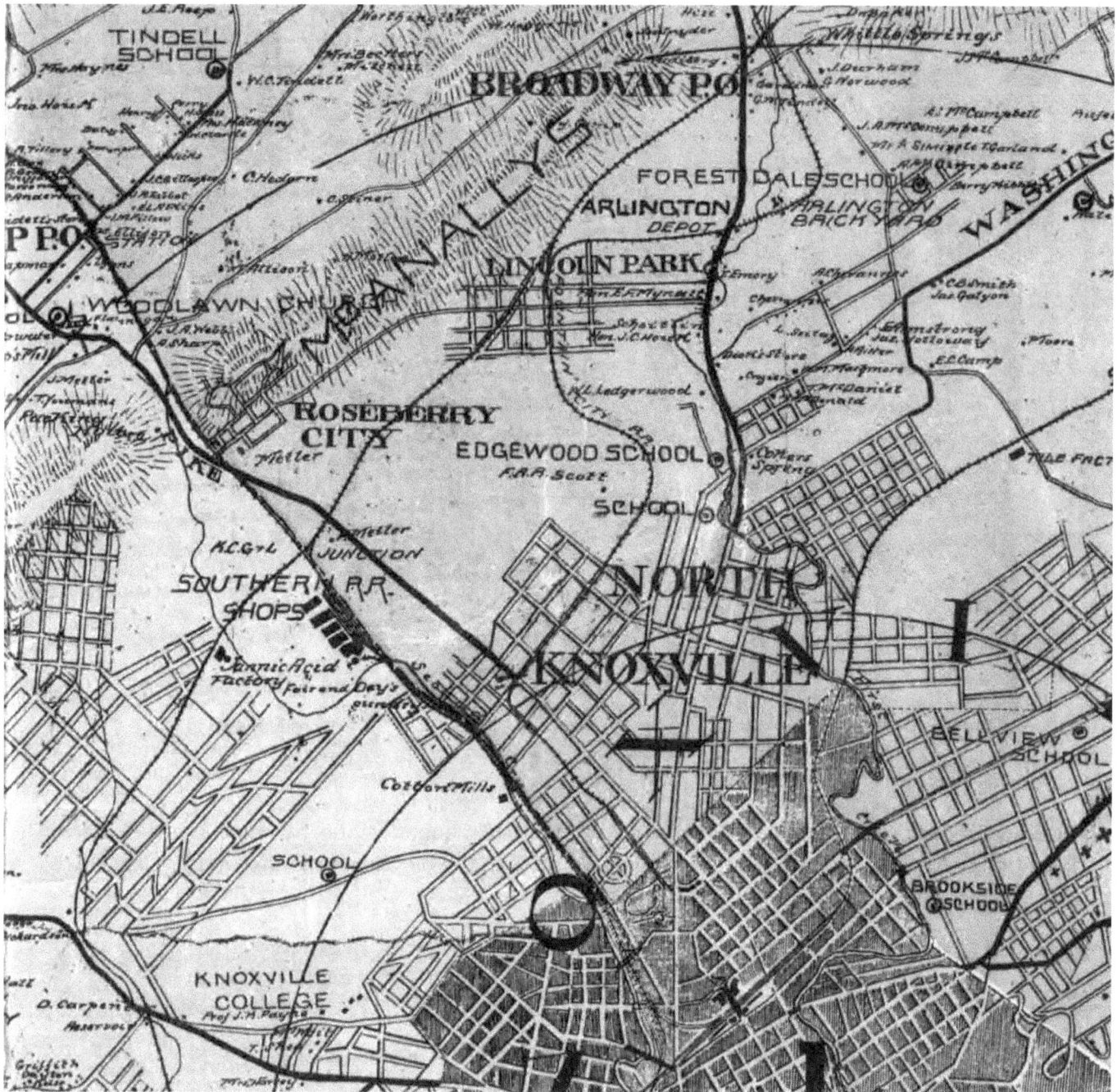

The Fountain City Dummy Line. The course of the Dummy Line came out of Knoxville up Jacksboro Street (present-day Cooper Street), past the Old Gray Cemetery, and circled around present day St. Mary's Hill (where the map indicates the home of F. A. R. Scott), then turned back to the west to bisect the original Lincoln Park development before heading east across Broadway at Walker Boulevard.

Also note from this 1895 map from the Library of Congress that the development of Lincoln Park was at least 10 years earlier than C.B. Atkin's Oakwood development. The map shows the original grid pattern development for the communities of Lincoln Park, Arlington (today the Fairmont Emoriland neighborhood) as well as the historically black Roseberry City community. Note some other interesting features included on this map: The homes of the Metlers, W.L. Ledgerwood (Cedar Grove), F.A.R Scott (St Mary's Hill), and the Scheitlins are visible on the map. Mrs. Churchwell's place near the railroad is conspicuously missing, although she would live another three years. Also, a brickyard existed at Arlington, Sharp's Ridge was called McAnally's, and the Edgewood School is visible, located in the present-day Broadway Shopping Center, at the approximate location of the Save-A-Lot food store. Further visible are the contours of First and Second Creek. *Map courtesy Library of Congress.*

End of an Era. The Knoxville streetcar line followed its serpentine course through Oakwood and Lincoln Park until its last run in July 1947. Here it circles a house on Chicamauga near Gilmer's filling station. *Photo courtesy Joe Bell.*

Dummy Lines and Streetcars

From its charter in 1889 until 1905 the original Fountain Head Railway, or "Dummy Line," a steam locomotive railway that alternately pulled open-air summer cars and closed passenger cars in winter, connected Knoxville to the resort community built around the Fountain Head Hotel in Fountain City at the corner of Hotel and Broadway. The Dummy Line began at the Central Market, known today as Emory Place, across Broadway from Old Gray Cemetery.

In the *Knoxville News-Sentinel* January 10, 1960, Lucy Curtis Templeton described the route:

> "It left town from a station on the corner on North Broadway and Holston (now Tyson) Street, which runs along the northern side of Old Gray Cemetery. … After the "dummy" left the station in town it puffed along Holston Street past the National Cemetery, past the old General Hospital, then due north until it came to what is now Woodland Ave. The area was a true woodland then; there was only one stop in the lovely grove after leaving the Foster Scotts. This stop was at the home of Mr. Eugene Mynders, about midway between the turn into Woodland and the next bend, which was on a hillside above Mucktown and below the F.A.R. Scott's large brick residence on top of the hill where St. Mary's Hospital now stands.

After some semi-circling south here, the 'dummy line' turned north once more, ran through Lincoln Park where there was a siding used to let one train pass another. … After leaving Lincoln Park, the line took a turn to the east, ran along what is now Walker Boulevard, and crossed Broadway at Arlington where there was a station. It then resumed its course along Walker Boulevard past the brickyard and then the Apple Tree Station on the McCampbell farm.

"… The line then turned north again past Whittle Springs through a pleasant meadow to Greenway, where there was another station. …From this point, the 'dummy' ran along the same route followed later by the streetcars and buses. The first streetcars did not go over Walker Boulevard. … From Greenway it was a straight shoot to Fountain Head. It was not until years later that North Broadway was extended along what had been the old 'dummy' line, although there might have been a side road there. The main highway ran to the right through Smithwood."

By 1905, the steam-driven Dummy Line was replaced with an electric streetcar line, which ran along the same route until 1947, when the advent of the personal automobile caused ridership on streetcar lines to sharply decline.

The Path of the Streetcar Line in Lincoln Park. Lincoln Park native Chris Hoosier has extensively photographed and studied the remnant paths of the the old streetcar line through Oakwood-Lincoln Park. Certain sections could offer connected walking trails through the community. *Photo courtesy Chris Hoosier.*

Solemn Journey. The streetcar makes its way down Chicamauga near the last cross street before Gilmer's filling station. *Photo courtesy Joe Bell.*

Last Days of the Streetcars. The Knoxville streetcar rounds the bend at Pershing Street and Chicamauga Avenue on July 15, 1947, in front of the Mobil gas station that Sam Gilmer Sr. built in 1932. *Photo courtesy Barbara and Bob Bailes.*

Part Two:
The People of Oakwood and Lincoln Park

West Drug Store. Interior of West Drug Store, corner of North Central and Burwell, most recently, the location of Steamboat Sandwiches. Clarence Cox worked as a pharmacist for Doc West here before operating Broadway Pharmacy at Broadway and Gill Street in the 1930s and 1940s. *Photo courtesy Larry Cox.*

At Work

While primarily small and humble, there have always been vital neighborhood businesses all up and down North Central Street, from the Old City to Sharp's Gap. From Central at Woodland northward, the business corridor of Oakwood and Lincoln Park continues to thrive, and offers more opportunities for the business community than ever. Industrial areas on West Springdale Avenue, at the Coster Yards, and on North Avenue where the C.B. Atkin factory and Van Gilder Glass used to be offer room for even larger businesses like Sysco Foods, employing hundreds.

The lessons of these hardworking early pioneers in business demonstrate the values of building a loyal customer following, taking care of your customers in good times and bad, and while a business, learning the value of becoming a core gathering place for the neighborhood at large.

Further to the south, city loan programs are making facade improvements possible to bring back the area around Broadway and Central, and such improvements are tangible and long-lasting. In Happy Holler, around North Central and East Anderson Avenue, new businesses are opening every month it seems, from hipster vegetarian restaurants to Aveda salons. The I-275 Corridor Study, available at www.knoxmpc.org, could prove vital to the continued growth and improvement of the residential and business community of Oakwood-Lincoln Park. Such growth will continue northward, connecting existing businesses to new ones and forever strengthening the fabric of the community. Where will *you* open *your* business?

Family Pharmacy. Oakwood resident Clarence Cox, 1015 Emerald Avenue, operated the Broadway Pharmacy at the corner of Broadway and Gill in North Knoxville. The display case from this pharmacy now stands at the Time Warp Tea Room in Happy Holler on North Central. *Photo courtesy Larry Cox.*

Sam Cook Service Station. The Sam Cook service station was located at North Central Street and Springdale Avenue. This photo taken circa 1940. At right: Sam Cook at work inside his service station at Central and Springdale circa 1930's His daughter Katherine Cook Thomas was born in 1934. *Photos courtesy Katherine Cook Thomas.*

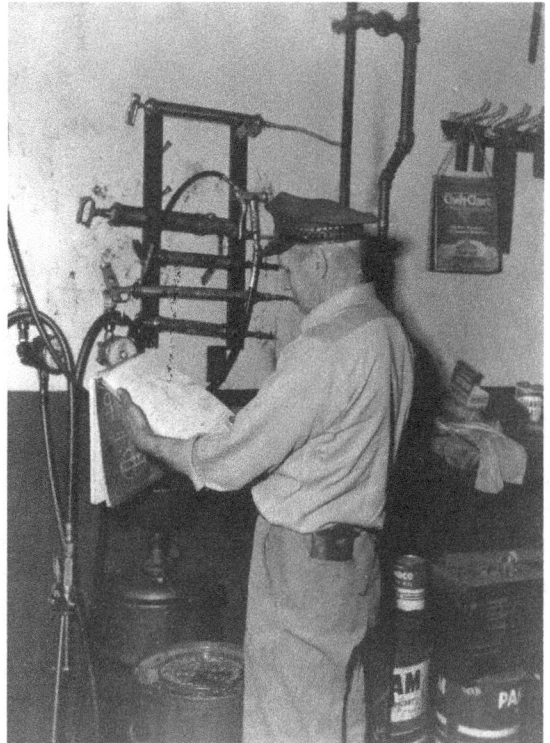

You've Dreamed Of A Perfect Service Station
PAN-AM AND SAM COOK HAVE BUILT IT FOR YOU
The Ultra Modern And Beautiful New
SAM COOK'S *Pan-Am* SERVICE STATION

2314 North Central at Springdale

Ample Parking Space

OPEN
7:30 A. M.
CLOSE
10 P. M.
7 DAYS A WEEK

Sam Cook's Pan-Am Station. Sam Cook built a new service station at Central and Springdale in the 1960's. While the original station from the 1930's was Sinclair Oil, he built his new station with Pan-Am. *Photo courtesy Katherine Cook Thomas.*

Knoxville Fire Station Number 8. Early photograph of Engine Co. Number 8, possibly 1930s, located on the south side of East Caldwell Avenue in the 300 block. The City of Knoxville Fire Department still operates its Arson Unit from this location. *Photo courtesy Larry Cox.*

Oscar Mayer Weiner Mobile. Albert Bridges poses with the "Little Oscar Chef" at Bridges Grocery, 2730 North Central, circa 1940s. *Photo courtesy Doris Bridges.*

Cloth workers, Brookside Mills. A group of cloth room workers at Brookside Mill circa 1910. Many Oakwood and Lincoln Park residents were employed at the knitting mills at Brookside Mills on Baxter Avenue and Standard Knitting Mills on Washington Avenue over in Park City. *Photo courtesy Edna Mae Frances Scarborough.*

And the band played on. A rare photograph of the Brookside Mills marching band circa 1920. *Photo courtesy Edna Mae Frances Scarborough.*

Reagan's Grocery. Fletcher L. Reagan opened his grocery store at 2400 North Central in Lincoln Park in 1920. Reagan's home was just to the south at 2314 Central Street. *Photo courtesy Fletcher Reagan.*

Reagan's Grocery on North Central Street. Exterior of Reagan's Grocery at 2400 North Central Street. Charles E. "Bus" Reagan bought the store from his father in 1940. Charles, born 1904 died 1980 was married to Thelma Shields Reagan. Right: Fletcher L. Reagan hosts a Reagan family reunion circa 1917 with many Reagan family members attending from Gatlinburg. *Photo courtesy Fletcher Reagan.*

Homer Hamilton's White Store No. 9. Homer Hamilton ran this White store for 34 years at 2501 North Central Street at Burwell Avenue. It was the first self service store in Knoxville. Keith Window Co. is located in that building today. *Photo courtesy Vernon Hamilton.*

Modern Grocery. Interior of Hamilton's White store at 2501 North Central Street. *Photo courtesy Vernon Hamilton.*

Homer Hamilton. Left: After a long day at work, Homer Hamilton enjoys dinner at home with his wife, Cora at what is today 319 Burwell Avenue. Above: Homer Hamilton, right, poses with a salesman inside his store. *Photo courtesy Vernon Hamilton.*

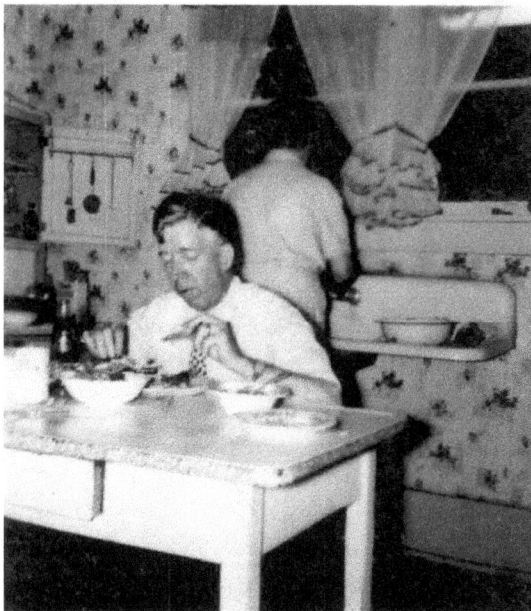

From Spaulding's Grocery to Historic Re-Use as The Parlor. Evelyn Spaulding, later Mrs. Walter Amman Jr., rides a bicycle in front of Grady Spaulding at his grocery on Chicamauga circa 1929-1934. Located at 726 Chicamauga, the building has been purchased by Josh Sidman and Rita Cochran, who are renovating it and plan to open the second location of The Parlor, a unique deli/coffee house with a music stage, sale and repair of vintage string instruments including guitars, mandolins, banjos, and basses, and music lessons. They grow their own produce in the garden behind this two-story brick building. Their first location is on Gay Street at the Knoxville Visitor's Center. *Photo courtesy Grady Amman.*

Sam Gilmer's Filling Station. Above: Two distinct views of Sam and Annie Gilmer's filling station at the intersection of Chicamauga and Pershing, a common gathering place in the Lincoln Park community by the 1930's and 40's. *Photo courtesy Ruth Ann Rogers and Ann Watson.*

Charles and Ruth Gilmer Leake. Left: Sam and Annie Gilmer's daughter Ruth married Charles Leake Jr. Here Charles and Ruth pose in front of the family business circa 1932. *Photo courtesy Ruth Ann Rogers and Ann Watson.*

Roy Sawyer's Barber Shop. Norma Kelley's father, Roy P. Sawyer had a barber shop next to Bailes meat market on the southeast corner of Central Street and Burwell Avenue. Roy Sawyer previously worked as a barber inside the Farragut Hotel in the 1930's. . *Photo courtesy Norma and Paul Kelley.*

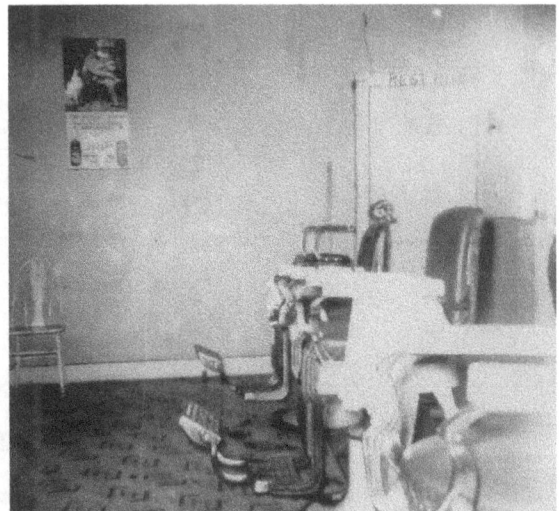

A Barber's Work is Never Done. Left: Roy Sawyer figures the receipts for the day at the Sawyer home 324 West Atlantic Avenue. Right: Inside Roy's barber shop at 2422 North Central Street. *Photo courtesy Norma and Paul Kelley.*

1963 Dodge Polara convertible

The Sawyers. Left: Roy Sawyer moved his barber shop from beside Baile's meat market next to 2422 North Central Street in the early 1960's. Right: Roy and Ethel Sawyer celebrate their 25th wedding anniversary in front of their fine Craftman's home at 324 West Atlantic Avenue. They paid $1900 for their house and proceeded to fill it full of furniture. *Photo courtesy Norma and Paul Kelley.*

Coming Soon: Bridges Grocery. Picture of Dixie Highway Service Garage on North Central with Albert Bridges and his daughters Trula and Doris outside of the store, right after he purchased the building in 1927. *Photo courtesy Doris Bridges.*

The Industrious Albert Bridges. Albert Bridges walking down Central with the old Esso sign behind. Note the difference in the neighborhood. *Photo courtesy Doris Bridges.*

Part of the Community. Inside Bridges Grocery. During the time that Albert S. Bridges and Ada Helen Morton Bridges operated their grocery at 2730 North Central, the store, like many of the stores along Central, were a big part of the community, just like the churches. According to Doris Bridges, the customers were all known by name and in the very beginning, her father, Albert, himself a veteran of World War I, felt a kinship with young boys leaving for the Second World War from Lincoln Park. As times changed, more and more people came into the store. Some walked, others drove their vehicles, and even the bus stopped at Bridges Grocery. It was normal for people to get off the bus from Knoxville, or ride their bicycles, and come straight into the store. The Bridges hired many young people while running the grocery store. Their hard work and dedication was always appreciated. *Photo courtesy Doris Bridges.*

Inside Bridges Grocery. Albert Bridges inside Bridges Grocery in front of the heating stove, taken soon after the display cases and coolers had been installed. Bridges Grocery looked like many other stores of the time. Shelves lined the walls, while tables filled the middle of the room and a coal stove heated the store. In the beginning, there was no refrigeration, so fresh vegetables, canned food, and dry goods were their main products. Fresh vegetables were always provided from local farmers' gardens. During the Great Depression, Albert Bridges would pick up the commodities down in Knoxville and bring them to the store for customers to pick up. Not everyone had a way to get to Knoxville to pick up their commodities, like rice, flour, sugar, coffee, and other items. Many customers stated that they would always trade with Mr. Bridges as long as he was in business, because he fed them during the Depression, when they had no money and no job with children to feed. Those customers were faithful to the end. Ada Bridges passed away in 1960, and Albert ran the store another three years, finally retiring and selling the store in 1963. His days were then filled puttering in his huge garden and taking fishing trips. He always stayed in touch with his neighbors and enjoyed seeing them when they stopped by to speak at the family home on Central. *Photo courtesy Doris Bridges.*

Oakwood School. Early photo of Oakwood School on Churchwell Avenue, near Saint Mary's Hospital, possibly 1920s. Pictured at left in front: teacher Elma Bishop. Also pictured is principal James Russell, seated in front. *Photo courtesy Knox County Two Centuries Photograph Project, McClung Historical Collection.*

At School

There is such a timelessness to our own years in school. We often feel that we are the first ones, the pioneers, that neither our teachers nor our parents really understand what school is like for "us."

This chapter reflects so many generations, from beloved teacher and principal Miss Helon Brixey, who passed away several years ago at the tender age of 104. The author had the pleasure of meeting her while working on a previous book about Park City, and the stories of Miss Brixey, from her imposing stature to her ability to fight for her school with the school administration and get it the resources it needed are indeed legend. There are many other beloved teachers reflected in this chapter, as well as many of the students who passed through Oakwood School, Lincoln Park School, and Christenberry Junior High School.

Worthy of mention too are Whittle Springs Middle and Fulton High School, which really deserve books of their own, but due to space limitations, could not really do these schools justice in a book about the entire Oakwood-Lincoln Park community. Many Oakwood-Lincoln Park kids also attended Old Knoxville High School and Central High School, making profiles of all of these schools more than cumbersome.

Perhaps another project for another day.

Future Pharmacist at Oakwood School.
Clarence Cox carries his schoolbooks to
Oakwood School, circa 1916 or 1917. *Photo
courtesy Larry Cox.*

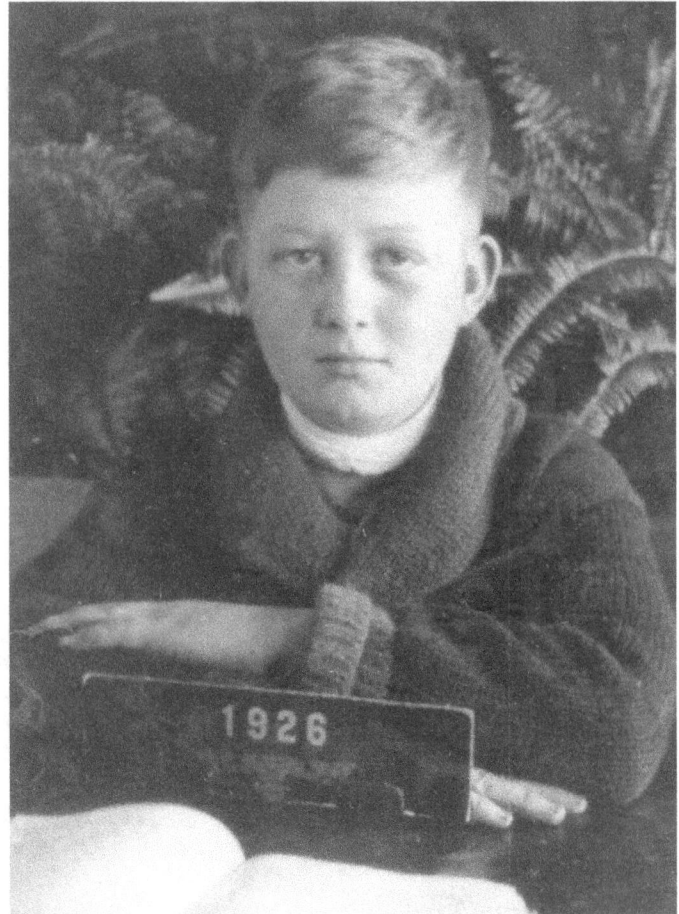

Future Postman at Lincoln Park School. 1926
image of Carroll Hassell at Lincoln Park School.
Photo courtesy Jennifer Montgomery.

Oakwood School Class. 1930s image of gold star pupils at Oakwood School. *Photo courtesy Cyndy Cox.*

Third and Fourth Grade, Oakwood School, 1915. 1915 image of Miss Hazell O'Dell's third and fourth grade classes. Clarence Cox is at the right end of the front row. His future wife Wille Mynatt Gibbs is second from right, second row. *Photo courtesy Larry Cox.*

Oakwood Outing. A group of Oakwood School students gather for an outing away from school, across the street from the present Oakwood School on East Churchwell Avenue. *Photo courtesy Larry Cox.*

"Knowledge is Power." 1949 combined first grade class of Miss Limberg and Miss Virgie Lane. They were beloved teachers, and a plaque on the front of the school facing Churchwell Avenue honors Miss Lane for her service to the school from 1923-1959. *Photo courtesy Larry Cox.*

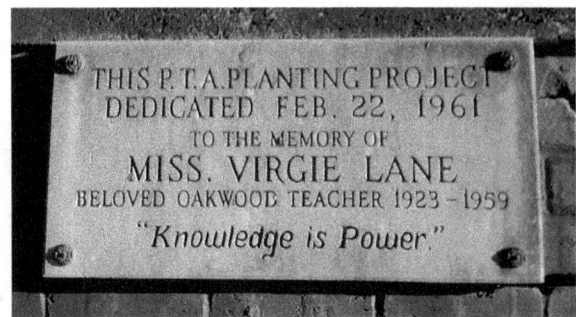

THIS P.T.A. PLANTING PROJECT
DEDICATED FEB. 22, 1961
TO THE MEMORY OF
MISS. VIRGIE LANE
BELOVED OAKWOOD TEACHER 1923 – 1959
"Knowledge is Power."

The Enchanted Runaways at Oakwood School. Four cast members of "The Enchanted Runaways," Oakwood School's play marking National Library Week, April, 1975. Players are from left: Teresa Breeden as "Sis," Jamie Lewis as "Mary Poppins," David Wood as "Travis Gibson," and John Kelley as "Bobby." *Photo courtesy Norma and Paul Kelley.*

Miss Limberg's First Grade at Oakwood School. Miss Limberg's 1948 first grade class at Oakwood School. *Photos courtesy Larry Cox.*

Christenberry Auditorium. A student ceremony in the auditorium at Christenberry Junior High School circa 1940's. *Photo courtesy Vernon Hamilton.*

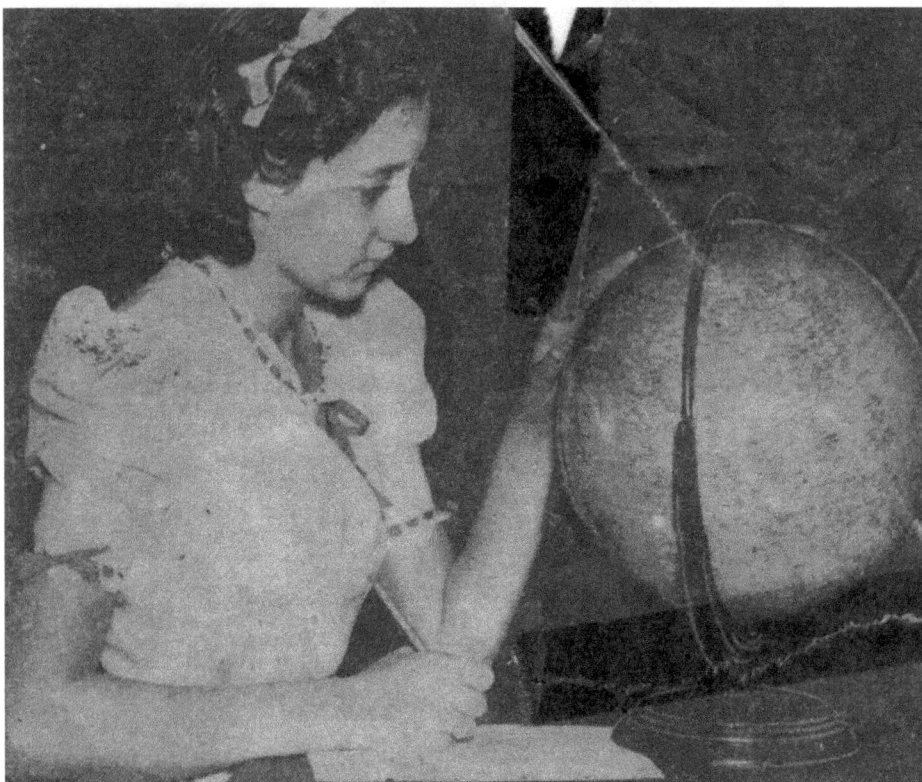

Christenberry Kid. Ann Gilmer, a 9th grader at Christenberry Junior High, consults the old standby, a world globe, for an English essay. In this 1920s image, Ann finds much of the map of Europe out of date. *Photo courtesy Ruth Ann Rogers and Ann Watson.*

Christenberry Basketball Team. The Christenberry Junior High basketball team circa 1961-1962. Coach Jerry Wrinkle. Front row: Joe McCarter, Stanley Mayes, Gordy Edmons, Sid Seals, Mike Fletcher. Second row, standing: Wilford Ownby, David Watson, Ed Clark, Len Sloan, Doug Leahy, Jackie Barry. *Photo courtesy Helen Kirby.*

Fulton High School Band. Performance of the Fulton High School band in the early 1970's. *Photo courtesy Marsha Robbins.*

Lincoln Park School. The view from Sam and Annie Gilmer's house at 520 Chicamauga Avenue overlooking students in front of Lincoln Park School, possibly 1940's. *Photo courtesy Ruth Ann Rogers and Ann Watson.*

Lincoln Park Nativity Play. The beauty and simplicity of the Nativity is shown in this scene from the Lincoln Park School Christmas Play, "The Bethlehem Christmas." A chorus of 75 voices supported a cast of 22 in the 1944 play. Pictured are Mary Lynn Gilmer and Jackie Hays. *Photo courtesy Norma and Paul Kelley.*

Fourth Grade at Lincoln Park School. Fourth grade class at Lincoln Park School in 1947. Second row third from left is Ruth Ann Leake Rogers. *Photo courtesy Ruth Ann Rogers and Ann Watson.*

Sixth Grade at Lincoln Park School. Sixth grade class at Lincoln Park School in 1948. Bill Rogers who would go on to marry Ruth Ann Leake is in the back row second from left. *Photo courtesy Ruth Ann Rogers and Ann Watson.*

Easter Program at Oakwood School. An adorable Easter program at Oakwood School in 1949. Left to right Barbara, Sue Barlow Newman, David, Nancy, Katheleen Fielden, Bobby Headder, and Gail Davis. *Photo courtesy Sue Newman.*

On Parade. Vernon Hamilton, a graduate of Old Knoxville High School, practices marching in his KHS band uniform around the neighborhood. According to Vernon, the band maintained its ROTC affiliation until 1949, four years after the end of World War II. *Photo courtesy Vernon Hamilton.*

Good Friends. Katherine Cook and Carol McIntyre pose on the new Christenberry Junior High playground/ballfield in the 1940's. They are still good friends to this day. *Photo courtesy Katherine Cook Thomas.*

Last Graduate Across the Stage at Old Knoxville High School. Norma Kelley (Sawyer) stands in cap and gown in front of the Sawyer home at 324 West Atlantic Avenue. Norma received the very last diploma awarded from Old Knoxville High School with the class of 1951. *Photo courtesy Norma and Paul Kelley.*

Christenberry Teachers. Two Teachers at Christenberry Junior High School on Class Day (Awards Day) 1960. English teacher John Pate and 7th grade English teacher Emma Jean Leek Huddleston. *Photo courtesy Emma Jean Leek Huddleston.*

Emma Jean Leek Huddleston. Miss Emma Jean Leek stands in front of mimosa trees at Christenberry Junior High School. She taught at Christenberry from 1954 to 1960 and at Whittle Springs Middle School from 1960 to 1965. She married Bill Huddleston. *Photo courtesy Emma Jean Leek Huddleston.*

Christenberry Junior High School Teachers, 1960. Front row: Mr. Bales, Mr. Davenport, Mr. Mills, Mr. Steinhoff, Mr. Underwood, Mr. Highbaugh, Mr. Dyer, Mr. (Paul) Kelley) and Mr. Parry. Second row: Mrs. Johnson, Mrs. Lewis, Mrs Yearwood, Miss Rennolds, Mrs. Morton, Mrs. Stringham, Miss Reynolds, Miss Banks, Mrs. Lebow, Mrs. Peterson, Mrs. Anderson, Mrs. Garrett, Mrs. Bromley, Mrs. Garrison, and Mrs. Phillips. Third row: Miss McPheeters, Mrs. Pinkston, Mrs. McPherson, Miss (Norma) Sawyer, Miss Peters, Miss Moody, Mrs. Siler, Miss (Helon) Brixey, Miss (Emma Jean) Leek, Miss Parrott, Miss Tudor, Mrs. Edwards, Miss Stoddard, Mrs. Briscoe, and Mrs. Haynes. *Photo courtesy Emma Jean Leek Huddleston.*

Christenberry Junior High School Exterior, 1968. Exterior of Christenberry Junior High School, 1968. *Photo courtesy Donnie Cathey.*

Oakwood School Wing Burns

Charred ruins of the inside of the rear wing of Oakwood School are shown in this picture of the early morning blaze, which caused probably $40,000 to $50,000 damage, but luckily the flames were confined to the rear portion of the building. Firemen are shown pouring water on the embers from the second floor.

Fire at Oakwood School. Several newspaper clippings detail a serious fire that occurred at Oakwood School in 1945 or 1946. *Photo courtesy Sam E. Bratton, Jr.*

School Fire Causes Loss of $50,000

Pre-Dawn Blaze at Oakwood Destroys Entire Back Wing

A spectacular pre-dawn blaze which gutted about one-third of Oakwood School gave some 600 elementary pupils an unexpected holiday today, and left school officials with the problem of how to place them in other already crowded schools. Two firemen were injured while fighting the flames.

Fire Chief Johnson said the fire apparently started in the boiler room, under the back wing of the building, and burned upwards. He estimated damage at about $50,000.

Only a portion of the total damage to the building will be covered by insurance, Finance Director Jack Burrows said. City schools are covered by policies which protect 70 to 80 per cent of the value of the buildings.

"We have no accurate estimate of the damage yet," Mr. Burrows said.

The firemen arrived on the scene at 5:40 a. m., and the fire had already enveloped the back wing of the three-story brick building.

"We were able to hold the fire within the back wing, and although flames ate out doors leading to the main or front section of the building, the fire never did get any further," Chief Johnson said. "It was a good piece of work by firemen keeping the fire confined like they did."

Flames had subsided at 7 a. m., but water was still being poured on the smouldering timbers of the rear section. Water and smoke damaged the front section, but not seriously, it was believed.

The section which burned contained the auditorium, several classrooms on the first floor, the cafeteria and storeroom, and the basement boiler room.

Two firemen, J. Otto Shetterly and Jim Tauscher, were injured when a concrete cornice fell as they were holding a hose into the basement, shortly after the department arrived on the scene.

Get Hip, Shoulder Injuries

Fireman Shetterly, 31, of Topside, received a severe hip injury, and Fireman Tauscher, 34, a newcomer to the Fire Department, who lives at 915 Calloway Street, has a shoulder injury. They were taken to General Hospital for treatment.

A janitor was reported to have discovered the blaze when he appeared for work, Principal I. T. Sliger said.

The brick building, located on East Churchwell Avenue, was built in 1914.

The flames destroyed an undetermined amount of foodstuffs in the cafeteria storeroom, including several dozen gallon cans of food.

Library Little Damaged

Fire made a blackened mass of the piano kept in the auditorium. The small library across the hall from the auditorium had little water damage. Five classrooms and several cloakrooms on the second floor escaped damage from both fire and water. Desks in a room, almost facing the auditorium, had been covered with tarpaulin by workers, been spraying with However, the water dam

Work of Repairing Oakwood School Is Begun Five Months After Fire Damaged Structure

Officials Blame Lapse on Failure To Settle Insurance

Work of repairing the Oakwood School finally was started today, almost exactly five months from the time the building was damaged by fire last March, but there was sharp disagreement in official circles on the reason for the long delay.

As a result of that delay it appeared today that at least two classes of elementary students will have to occupy basement rooms during the fall and winter months, and that one or more classes may have to be moved to some other building, although school officials say that may not be necessary.

School Board Chairman Forest Andrews, Supt. Tom C. Prince and Business Manager E. L. Adcock all said today the delay was caused by failure of insurance companies to adjust the loss caused by the fire and make the insurance payment.

Says Money Available

On the other hand, City Finance Director Jack Burrows said, that although the insurance money has not been collected, sufficient money to make the repairs at Oakwood is available and has been available in special city funds since the date of the fire.

"The money is available in both the city's school replacement fund and in the 5-cent school building levy fund," Mr. Burrows said. "We have not received an insurance settlement, but the money on hand could have been used at any time and replaced after the insurance money is paid."

The repair work was started after the School Board last night ordered part of the damaged building abandoned and authorized construction of an addition to replace it. The part to be torn down is that part of the top floor formerly used as an auditorium.

Temporary Roof Built

After the fire a temporary roof was built over the auditorium floor to protect classrooms below. That roof now is to be replaced with a permanent roof and the fire-blackened walls of the auditorium are to be removed.

Mr. Andrews said today that "part of the reason" for the long delay in starting repairs was the lack of money because the insurance had not been adjusted. Mr. Andrews, at home suffering with a severe throat infection, said he was unable to discuss the matter further today.

Mr. Prince said he "understood" from reports by the business manager that the delay was caused by failure to collect the insurance.

"It seems to me that it has been a mighty long delay," Mr. Prince commented, "but I understand from the business manager that the work has been delayed be-

These broken walls of the former second-floor auditorium at Oakwood School were being removed today as work finally was started on repairs to the building, which was damaged by fire last March. Parents of Oakwood pupils had protested that these walls were a hazard for children both inside and outside of the building.

Fire at Oakwood School. Several newspaper clippings detail a serious fire that occurred at Oakwood School in 1945 or 1946. *Photo courtesy Sam E. Bratton, Jr.*

Schmoozing for Her School. Miss Helon Brixey, left, principal of Christenberry Junior High School, knew how to gather the resources she needed for her school. In this 1954 photo, she is hosting a dinner at the school for Knoxville mayor George Dempster, Mr. New, the superintendent of city schools and Mr. Gentry, the Director of Instruction for the Knoxville City Schools. *Photo courtesy Norma and Paul Kelley.*

Miss Mattie Hammer, Lincoln Park School. Miss Mattie Hammer, above, was a much loved teacher at Lincoln Park School. She taught Ruth Gilmer, daughter of Sam and Annie Gilmer in the 1920's. *Photo courtesy Ruth Ann Rogers and Ann Watson.*

Underwood, Educator, Dies At 87

Rufus H. Underwood, former city school principal, one-time mayor of Oakwood, and a leading Baptist churchman, died Wednesday morning at Fort Sanders Presbyterian Hospital. He was 87.

Mr. Underwood suffered a stroke 11 years ago.

Although his weakened condition continued, he was in fine mental state and talked with interest to his nurses and those who called for visits at his bedside. He was given a surprise birthday dinner at his hospital room on his 87th birthday.

Before his health failed rapidly, Mr. Underwood was active in church work. He taught a Bible class at First Baptist where he was a member. He was interested in all departments of the church and Baptist Brotherhood Work.

He began his career as an educator in Anderson County and later came to Knoxville in 1902 and taught in Knox County rural schools. He was a native of Anderson County and was graduated from Holbrook Normal College (now Central High School) in 1889 and then studied at University of Tennessee.

Mr. Underwood served as principal of South Knoxville and Brownlow grammar schools. He was at Brownlow in 1940 when he retired.

He is survived by a son by a former marriage, Brig. Gen. (ret.) Edgar H. Underwood, of Bradenton, Fla.; a sister, Mrs. J. C. Hill, Cunningham Road; and grandsons, Col. Edgar Underwood Jr. Orlando, Fla., and Robert Underwood, Tampa, Fla.

The body was removed to Mann's Mortuary. Funeral arrangements were incomplete last night.

Mayor and Principal. In addition to serving as Mayor of Oakwood, Rufus Underwood was also a principal in the Knoxville City School System at South Knoxville and Brownlow elementary schools. *Photo courtesy Edna Mae Frances Scarbrough.*

Mrs. Hutchins, Lincoln Park School. Mrs. Hutchins, left, taught fourth grade at Lincoln Park School. *Photo courtesy Harold Elkins.*

Miss Emma Jean Leek, Christenberry Junior High School. Miss Emma Jean Leek, faculty photograph. *Photo courtesy Emma Jean Leek Huddleston.*

Miss Bright. Miss Bright poses happily in front of her shiny new 1953 Plymouth Cranbrook. She taught third grade at Lincoln Park School. *Photo courtesy Harold Elkins.*

Miss Norma Sawyer (Kelley.) Norma Kelley sits at her desk grading papers at Christenberry Junior High School. She taught reading and 8th and 9th grade English before becoming the librarian at Whittle Springs Middle School from 1963 to 1993. *Photo courtesy Norma and Paul Kelley.*

Fulton High School Basketball. Fulton High School basketball team, Coach Mike Adkins. *Photo courtesy Norma and Paul Kelley.*

Fulton High School Student Writes the Theme Song to the 1982 Knoxville World's Fair. John Kelley, son of Norma and Paul Kelley, writes the winning song for the 1982 Knoxville World's Fair. *Photo courtesy Norma and Paul Kelley.*

Fulton Senior Tunes Into Fair With Top Song

John Kelley, a senior at Fulton High School, has won the contest for writing the city's official song for the World's Fair and the song has also been selected as the official song for use by the World's Fair.

Kelley, president of the student council, is the son of Dr. and Mrs. Paul Kelley. The father is assistant superintendent of city schools for instruction.

Kelley

The contest for the city's song was open to city school students who wrote words and simple accompaniment. The winner — "To Turn the World" — was chosen by singer Ray Stevens.

Rick Paulus, a sophomore at Bearden High School and son of Dr. and Mrs. Thomas J. Paulus, was second-place winner. The third-place winner was Barry Wallace, a sophomore at Central High and son of Mr. and Mrs. Dennis M. Wallace.

The song has been copyrighted by the city and recorded on Vasari Records. It was submitted to Knoxville International Energy Exposition (KIEE), developer of the World's Fair, for consideration as the official World's Fair song.

Fair executives today said the song would be the one officials use for the fair.

The mayor's office and Hewgley's Music Shop sponsored the contest. Hewgley's provided the prizes of $100 for first place, $75 for second place and $50 for third.

Lincoln Park Methodist Church. The original Lincoln Park Methodist Church was located on Pershing Avenue. The image is of the Men's Sunday School class, sometime between 1910 and 1916. Mr. Strange, the teacher, is at the far right. The names provided are from the back of the photo, and not all present are named. Front row l-r: Clifford Davis, Roy Gilmer, Percy Gilmer, Herbert Davis, Lee Sullenberger. Second row, l-r: Eugene Henderson, Bob Webb, Walter Amman, Floyd Larue, Charlie Hammond, Floyd Brown. Third row l-r: unknown, John Hoskins, Charlie Kalthproof, unknown, Be Kropff, Mr. Harris. *Photo courtesy Grady Amman.*

Churches

Early churches were Oakwood Methodist Episcopal on Springdale Avenue, founded at an earlier mission site of Second Presbyterian Church in 1906. The present church is located on Burwell Avenue. It was built in 1926. Oakwood Baptist Church was also founded as a mission with its roots growing from a five room house on the corner of Burwell and Harvey which was remodeled into Sunday School rooms. The church was organized on May 28, 1905 with the charter members coming from Broadway Baptist which was called Calvary Baptist. Its name was changed to Oakwood Baptist when it relocated to Columbia Avenue in 1910. A Methodist church was located on the fringe of Oakwood. It began as McMillan Chapel as a a Sunday School in 1892. It was a missionary outreach of Centenary Methodist Episcopal Church, South. It was located at 135 East Emerald Avenue. In 1903, it was joined with Lincoln Park Methodist Episcopal Church South for two years. In 1930 McMillan Chapel, founded 1904-05, became Emerald Avenue Methodist Episcopal Church South and located on the corner of Emerald and Central. Churches and choirs were an integral part of the community and church bells chimed on Sunday mornings and special occasions.

Lynwood United Methodist Church at 119 Cedar Avenue. This church dates to circa 1919-1922, when David Wichser , M. O. Summers, W. C. Rector, F. G. Scott, W. M. McIntyre, J. Boyd McCalla and Partin Moore became trustees of Roseberry Methodist Episcopal Church, South. *Photo courtesy Norma and Paul Kelley.*

Atlantic Avenue Missionary Baptist Church. Pastored by Eddie Seals, the church is located at 401 Atlantic Avenue. Sermons are available on www.atlanticavebaptist.com. *Photo courtesy Norma and Paul Kelley.*

Outreach Baptist Church. A primitive Baptist church located at 401 Cedar Avenue, known for its outdoor church singings. *Photo courtesy Norma and Paul Kelley.*

Lincoln Park Methodist Church. 3120 Pershing Street. *Photo courtesy Park City Press.*

Lincoln Park United Methodist Church

In 1903, Lincoln Park was a heavily wooded section with dirt and gravel streets. The old street car line had not been extended as far as Lincoln Park. The number of families in the area was beginning to grow, and several families exhibited Methodist leanings. The Hungerfords, Seatons and Stranges all lived within calling distance of each other on Chicamauga Avenue, and in the evenings, they would gather on the porches of one of the houses and talk about what it would mean to begin a Methodist congregation in the area.

After discussing it with their friends, on October 3, 1903, they met on the porch of Mr. and Mrs. M. M. Hungerford at what was then 725 Chicamauga Avenue. The following Thursday, Dr. C. O. Jones, Presiding Elder, met with the leaders, and the following Sunday, the organization was formed at the old County School House at the corner of Atlantic Avenue and Kenyon Street.

Charter families included Mr. and Mrs. C. S. Adams, Mr. and Mrs. G. W. Bartlett, Mrs. John Faulkner, Mr. and Mrs. Ed Hammond, Mr. and Mrs. J. P. Henry, Mr. and Mrs. M. M. Hungerford, Mr. and Mrs. P. D. Roady, Mr. and Mrs. Charles E. Seaton, Mr. and Mrs. George C. Heap Sr., Mrs. W. P. Bean, Mrs. Elizabeth Matthews, J. S. Johnson, H. G. Price, Mr. and Mrs. Alexander Scott, and Mr. and Mrs. Joe. T Strange. At the October 12, 1903 session of the Holston Methodist Conference, held in Morristown, Lincoln

Park and McMillan's Chapel (now Emerald Avenue Methodist) were united in a mission, and the Rev. Charles T. Davis was appointed "preacher in charge."

The first year, all church meetings were held in the two-room County School House on Atlantic Avenue, and every Saturday morning, a "Bucket Brigade" of mothers and children armed with pails, soap, mops, and brooms went to the school and cleaned it up for Sunday services. They cleaned it again on Sunday afternoon for the school children on Monday.

In 1905, The Edgewood Land and Improvement Company, W.B. Mitchell, president, and J.C. White, secretary, donated a 75-foot lot on Willow Street (now Pershing) and a campaign began to pay for a new church. The cost of the first building was approximately $1,500. Dr. Emory Hawk, pastor of Broad Street Methodist Church at the corner of Broadway and Fifth Avenue in Knoxville, delivered the first sermon in the new building. In that first year, membership exceeded 100 people, and the debt was reduced to $800.

The first church was dismantled in March 1926, and construction began on the present brick church. The church met at Lincoln Park School during construction. Over the years, the small church has always had an ecumenical flavor. When a small Presbyterian Church in the community disbanded, many of those congregants joined Lincoln Park Methodist. This church also helped in the formation of other churches, including Brookside, Trinity, and Roseberry, which is now known as Lynnwood.

Lincoln Park Baptist Church. 830 Chicamauga Avenue. *Photo courtesy Park City Press.*

Lincoln Park Baptist Church

Lincoln Park Baptist Church was begun February 14, 1909, being organized in the Odd Fellows Hall on Chicamauga Avenue, according to the *Daily Journal and Tribune*. That same day, the Lincoln Memorial was being dedicated in Hodgenville, Kentucky, race riots were occurring in Louisville and Pittsburgh, William Jennings Bryan was on a southern speaking tour, and Tennessee Military Institute (TMI) beat the University of Tennessee in basketball 21-20.

Like Lincoln Park Methodist, their early meetings were also in the Old County School House on Atlantic Avenue. Charter members were: C. E. Buckles, Stella Buckley, J. B. Hicks, W. B. Goins, G. S. Bryan, E. W Ferguson, J. A. Wilson, J. W. Smith, Frank Sanders, Martha Wilson, Will Wilson, Jennie Hicks, J. J. Gillenwaters, Alice Gillenwaters, James B. Lovelace, Mary Davidson, Carrie Dowell, Hannah Dowell, J. W. Brown, C. W. Buckles, Hannah Ferguson, Fannie McCloud, F. F. Dowell, Bennie MeHaffey, Mrs. W. H. Allen, Mrs. G. S. Bryan, Mrs. M. J. Stern, Oran Ferguson, Mrs. W. B. Goins, Bessie McGill, J. F. Hodge, W. H. Bailey, Edith Kropff, J. W. Kropff, and Mary Yeatman.

Soon after the church began, the women organized their own organization, first called Willing Workers. They later became known as the Women's Missionary Society.

The church built its first building at 706 Chicamauga in 1910. An addition was built next to it in 1913. The next building, Templeton Chapel, was built in 1928 at a cost of $30,000. In 1932, it was partially destroyed by fire but was immediately rebuilt. The present auditorium was added in 1952-1953, along

117

with three floors of classroom space. The auditorium was first used on the second Sunday of February, 1953, on the 44th anniversary of the church. Despite six inches of snow, there were over 1300 in Sunday School.

In 1954-1955, the church added the Annex, which at the time cared for a Young People's Department and an Adult Department. In 1963, the church added the two-story west wing.

Oakwood Methodist Church. 334 East Burwell Avenue. *Photo courtesy Park City Press.*

Oakwood United Methodist Church

In the spring of 1906, 16 men and women from Oakwood met with Dr. George Thomas Francisco, the district superintendent of the Methodist Church for the Knoxville area. Francisco, born in the Solitude community of Hawkins County in 1868 and the great-great uncle of the author of this book, also met with the Rev. W. F. Pitts, pastor of East Main Church, and Mr. W. L. DeRieux, to seek help in establishing Oakwood Methodist Church.

Early church records indicate the following people as charter members: Mr. and Mrs. C. L. Barker, Mr. and Mrs. W. T. Beeler, Mrs. Fannie Steel, Alice Carter, Mrs. Lettie Stewart, Mr. Henson, Mr. and Mrs. D. B. Lewis, Mr. and Mrs. T. P. Duff, Mr. and Mrs. Thomas A. Pettit, Mrs. J. W. Line, and Mr. J. M. Shetterly.

Shortly thereafter, the group began negotiations with Second Presbyterian Church to purchase a chapel building in the 300 block of East Springdale Avenue, which had been used as a Presbyterian mission. The members of Oakwood Methodist Church purchased their first building on June 30, 1906 at a cost of $800.

Rev. Charles M. Davis, a local supply minister, was appointed to serve the church until a meeting of the conference. The congregation continued to grow, and during the pastorate of Rev. E. R. Branam, 1912-1914, a parsonage was purchased and the original building renovated. In 1919, Rev. W. M. McTeer led the congregation in acquiring the present property at 334 Burwell Avenue. The building committee included A. C. Lewis, P. P. Mynatt, W. R. Anderson, J. B. Cox, and Mark A. Scarbrough, Sr.

Using the architectural plans of Baumann and Baumann, architects in Knoxville, the project was approved by the church and Lynn A. Hayes, (see page 168) a Lincoln Park building contractor, was given a $50,000 contract to build the church. Work was begun in the summer of 1922 and the basement was completed in 1923, where the church worshipped for two years. The sanctuary was completed in 1926, and on Sunday, January 23, 1926, Dr. James M. Melear, editor of the *Christian Advocate* of the Holston Methodist Conference, delivered the first sermon in the new church.

During the Great Depression beginning in 1929, and into the early 1930s, the church, like many across the nation and in the neighborhood, faced economic hardships. but under the leadership of Rev. E. E. Cavaleri, negotiations with Fidelity Bankers Trust Co. kept the church out of bankruptcy and foreclosure. A successful financial campaign after near-foreclosure avoided this catastrophe.

In 1939, the women of the church formed a Women's Missionary Society, as well as during World War II, a Wesleyan Service Guild was organized for employed women. After many of these women retired in the late 1960s, the group disbanded.

Oakwood Baptist Church. Oakwood Baptist Church at 111 East Columbia Avenue. *Photo courtesy Park City Press.*

Oakwood Baptist Church

The Oakwood Baptist Church had its beginnings in a mission Sunday School sponsored by Broadway Baptist Church in 1903. The first meeting place was a little store building on Springdale Avenue, just west of North Central. Mr. Rufus H. Underwood became superintendent of the Sunday School and served well for more than 20 years at three locations. Mr. Underwood was also mayor of the City of Oakwood from 1913-1917, the entire life of the City, and was also principal of Oakwood School.

The Sunday School soon outgrew its small quarters and the church purchased two lots from Clay Brown Atkin, the developer of Oakwood, on the corner of Burwell Avenue and Harvey Street. Here a five-room home with the partitions removed was used for Sunday School and worship services.

The congregation was organized into a church May 28, 1905, by the Broadway Baptist Church and named Calvary Baptist Church. Rev. W. A. Atchley, pastor of Broadway, Rev. R. J. Medaris, pastor of South Knoxville Baptist, and Rev. A. J. Moore were members of the organizing council.

Rev. J. W. Crowe, a young student at Carson Newman College, became the first pastor of the church and served until 1908. In 1906, the name of the church was changed from Calvary to Oakwood Baptist Church to avoid confusion with another congregation of the same name.

When the church first considered a building program, it was decided that the present location was too close to Lincoln Park Baptist Church, so in 1910, lots were purchased on East Columbia Avenue, the present location of the church. Under the direction of Pastor George W. Edens, the Oakwood Baptist Church builts its first permanent home.

The church had difficulty in those early years raising the money for the new building, meeting current expenses, and giving to missions. But by 1930, under Brother C. L. Hammond, the membership had reached 600, and the growth of the church was solely funded by free-will offerings. All other fundraising approaches were abandoned. By 1937, the church, again feeling growing pains, raised $25,000 to build the new auditorium.

Brother Charles Ausmus became pastor in 1942, healing a split of the church which led approximately 50 members to leave and form Churchwell Avenue Baptist Church. The church continued to grow, and a third building program for the educational building was completed in 1946.

Oakwood Baptist Church, now 105 years old continues its mission into its second hundred years.

Emerald Avenue Methodist Church. 1620 North Central Street. *Photo courtesy Park City Press.*

Emerald Avenue United Methodist Church

Emerald Avenue Methodist Church was the first church in Oakwood, and grew out of a Sunday School program taught by a volunteer from Centenary Methodist Episcopal Church, South, under a brush arbor in the early 1890s.

The first church, a small frame building, was constructed at the northwest corner of Emerald Avenue and McMillan Street. First called McMillan Chapel, the name was changed to Emerald Avenue Methodist Episcopal Church, South, reflecting the separation of the denomination in 1844. Lincoln Park Methodist was also a "Southern" church, while Oakwood Methodist was Oakwood Methodist Episcopal Church (Northern). In 1903, Lincoln Park Methodist and McMillan Chapel were joined in a two-point circuit and remained joined for two years.

A substantial brick church on Emerald Avenue, facing North Central Street, was dedicated in 1932, during the height of the Great Depression. Unable to pay the mortgage payments, many members moved their membership, leaving a few to carry the financial load. In 1938, the lender foreclosed, and the property was auctioned on the steps of the Knox County Courthouse. It was bought by a few members, some of whom pledged their homes to protect the church.

Saved from the brink, the church once again began to grow, but like many urban churches, faced new challenges as more families moved to the suburbs and away from the center city. In the 1980s, a consultant from the Holston Methodist Conference advised church leaders to "reach out" to the community or "die as a church." Reacting to that advice, Pastor Robert H. "Bob" Bean and a young Maryville College graduate, Steve Diggs, employed part-time as a youth worker, recommended a radical course of action—a urban youth ministry project that today is one of the most successful and relevant urban ministries in East Tennessee and a model for outreach into the community.

The Emerald Youth Foundation (EYF), incorporated in 1991, is a non-denominational, urban children and youth ministry located at 1718 North Central Street in Oakwood-Lincoln Park.

The ministry grew out of a vision of Emerald Avenue United Methodist Church in 1988 to serve young people in the low to moderate income community of Oakwood-Lincoln Park in North Knoxville. In 1999, the Emerald Youth Foundation started a youth leadership development ministry that is now called JustLead. Their mission is to raise up a large number of just leaders who love Jesus Christ and others, maintain good health, and use their knowledge, skills, and gifts to renew their neighborhoods. Through JustLead and other ministry opportunities, Emerald Youth Foundation continues to serve young people via a growing network of urban churches in the Knoxville area.

For more about the sacrifice of one particular family who belonged to Emerald Avenue Methodist Church and their legacy to the Emerald Youth Foundation, see page 215.

First Baptist Church of Roseberry City. 217 Hiawassee Avenue. *Photo courtesy Park City Press.*

First Baptist Church of Roseberry City

Roseberry City is a historically black community of obscure origins that lies at the foot of Sharp's Ridge to the west of Lincoln Park and north of the old Linwood residential development east of Central Avenue, also known as Lynwood and also Lynnwood. At least three residential additions to "Linwood" began east of Metler Street, south of Chicamauga, continuing four blocks south to include Cedar Avenue, Atlantic Avenue, and Preston Avenue. The second addition continued west to Central Avenue, and the third addition added about 25 more residential lots west of Central Avenue over to the deep curve of the Southern Railway tracks. The area descending from the ridge down toward Atlantic and Preston Avenue is clearly marked as Roseberry City on an 1895 map of Knox County (see page 67), but the origin of the name is uncertain, and some of the Linwood area blurs with the historic Roseberry City.

To many, Roseberry City is considered part of Lincoln Park, but to some of the residents, it will always be distinct. The origins of the name Roseberry may refer back to at least 1874, when Roseberry's Creek "rises in Beaver Ridge, flows south-east, cutting through McAnnally's Ridge (today Sharp's Ridge)," according to the 1874 book, *Introduction to the Resources of Tennessee, Volume One,* by Joseph Buckner Killebrew.

There is another Roseberry Creek in the Mascot section of East Knox County, along with another Roseberry Baptist Church dating back to 1890. A William Roseberry purchased 300 acres north of the Holston River from Charles M. McClung in this area in 1798, but this is the only known early resident named Roseberry who bought or sold land in Knox County. In addition, a Thomas Roseberry had land in Anderson County in 1805.

First Baptist Church of Roseberry City was chartered October 1, 1915, according to a marble plaque on the side of the building at its present location at 217 Hiawassee Avenue, with the wooded mount of Sharp's Ridge rising dramatically behind it. Pastor E. H. Hamblin was the organizing pastor. Roy Jett, a long-time deacon who helped re-locate and re-build the church in 1952, once recalled a man who stopped their church van and asked, "Tell me where this Roseberry Baptist Church is. My mother says that there is such a place, but no one can tell me where it is!"

Pastors since Rev. Hamblin include J. H. Johnson, A. Nichols, T. S. Gordon, H. T. Fortson, H. S. Upton, W. H. Walker, C. L. Willis Sr., O. W. Willis, R. E. James, and current pastor W. L. Ghosten.

A more common name for the area, according to a church history, is Buzzard's Roost. "There was a slaughter pen (Metler's Abatoire) across the railroad tracks nearby and the carcasses of pigs were hauled way up on the ridge. Well, the buzzards would get wind of those carcasses and would just swarm the ridge," the story goes. "Although Sharp's Ridge is no longer littered with the carcasses of pigs and the buzzards have ceased to fly, that name continues to plague our community!"

The church was originally located on much steeper ground. In the 1943 Knoxville City Directory, it was located at 209 Watauga Avenue, a very steep location indeed. Roy Jett bid on a piece of delinquent property next to his house on Hiawassee for $150, but during this late period of a still-segregated Knoxville, a white bidder named Martin Hurray ran up the bid to make a profit, but Jett was successful with a final bid of $250. The church was deeded the land in only two years.

Prior to integration, children in Roseberry City were often required to go to work to support their family, and rarely finished elementary or high school. But according to the church, this lack of education did not prevent them as adults from providing for their families. Two women in the community, Mrs. Rooks and her daughter Mattie Rooks both finished college and became school teachers.

By the 1960s, the children of Roseberry City were integrated into Lincoln Park Elementary School. Many of their parents were worried that their children might be hurt, so they accompanied the kids to school when it was first opened to blacks. But a white co-worker assured "Mr. Roy" that the children would indeed be welcomed with open arms. "They were welcomed, too," he said. "There wasn't a bit of trouble."

Centerpointe Baptist Church. 2909 North Broadway. *Photo courtesy Park City Press.*

Centerpointe Baptist Church

Second Baptist Church began in 1969 as a series of weekly prayer meetings by a small, committed group of people from Oakwood-Lincoln Park. As this faith community grew, they added times for Bible study and for fellowship, and Paul Huling was the first minister to preach to this church. Gerald Brown served as interim pastor from November 1969 until June 1971, when Thomas Gatton became the first full-time pastor. Upon his retirement, Carl Simmons, Jr. serverd as pastor from 1992-2000. Greg Brewer was pastor from 2001-2002, and Dave Mason became the present pastor in 2003. Even on a weekday morning, one can often find the parking lot of this vibrant church nearly full.

The first official workship service for Second Baptist Church was held February 16, 1969 at Christenberry Junior High School, under a blanket of snow and hazardous driving conditions. A group of 94 people attended, and even one young girl publicly professed her faith at that first church service.

The group quickly named themselves Second Baptist Church, and 166 people became charter members. The church affiliated witht the Knox County Association of Baptists and the Southern Baptist Convention. That first year, the church purchased 2.5 acres of land at the present site at 2909 North Broadway, which included a large home which the church members renovated to meet their needs at the time. In 1972, the church broke ground for a three-story building for worship and educational space. The church acquired additional land from five adjacent properties to bring the total property to 4.3 acres. A larger worship center was built and dedicated on December 10, 1989.

In March, 2009, the church changed its name from Second Baptist Church to Centerpointe Baptist Church to better reflect the church's vision: "centered on Christ, pointed to our world, and connecting with people."

Womanless Wedding. A womanless wedding at Emerald Avenue Methodist church circa 1940's. Pictured are Jack Kidwell and Bob Payne. Others are unknown. *Photo courtesy Mary Jean Laugherty Larison and Carolyn Overton.*

Betty Keck Roach. Betty Keck Roach stands in front of Oakwood Baptist Church in this 1940's image. *Photo courtesy Lib Peters McCluskey.*

Methodist Men. The men of Oakwood Methodist Church pose in front of this building in this 1930's photo.. *Photo courtesy Mary Solomon.*

Bridges Sisters at Easter. Trula and Doris Bridges dressed up on Easter Sunday. *Photo courtesy Doris Bridges.*

Lincoln Park Methodist Kids. This 1920's image shows the many cute kids of Lincoln Park Methodist Church. *Photo courtesy Ann Watson.*

Charles Ausmus. Pastor Charles Ausmus, long-time pastor of Lincoln Park Baptist Church. He also pastored at Oakwood Baptist Church in the 1940s. *Photo courtesy Ethel Viles.*

Easter at Emerald Avenue Methodist. 1950 or 1951 image of Jerry Messer Green, Bill Gibbs, Larry Gibbs Cox, Bill Keith, father of Voice of the Vols/now Voice of the Tennessee Titans Mike Keith, Madeline Saylor Large, and Mike Messer. *Photo courtesy Larry Cox.*

The "Petticoat Church." Group of Emerald Avenue Methodist Women, who really became the backbone of the church and began running many of its functions by the 1940s. First row: Eula Gibbs, Nina Ridenour, Mrs. Statum. Second row: Mrs. W. F. Pate (standing), Lucille Wood, Mrs. Benny Hale, Mrs. W. H. Taylor, Mrs. Lula Acuff. Third row: Eula Huff, Martha Stansbury, unknown, Bertie Leek, unknown. *Photo courtesy Larry Cox.*

Emerald Avenue Methodist Missionary Society. The women of Emerald Avenue Methodist Church's Missionary Society now the United Methodist Women. In this 1928 photo, among others are Helen West Loula Acuff, and Willie Baldock. *Photo courtesy Biddy Leahy.*

Women's Missionary Society. Ada Bayless, president, Lorene Sharpe, vice president, and Emily Keith, secretary/treasurer of the 1959 Women's Missionary Society of the little church in the 400 block of Atlantic Avenue and McMurray. *Photo courtesy Harold Elkins.*

Oakwood Methodist Church. Women of Oakwood Methodist Church, circa 1940s. *Photo courtesy Mary Solomon.*

Interior of Oakwood Methodist Church. Interior of Oakwood Methodist Church. *Photo courtesy Vernon Hamilton.*

Easter at Oakwood Baptist Church. Easter at Oakwood Baptist Church, circa 1960s. Shirley and Jack Ivester, Mr. and Mrs. Jack Kerr. *Photo courtesy Kermit Kitts.*

After Church at Oakwood Baptist Church. A group of women gather outside Oakwood Baptist Church at the corner of east Columbia and North Central. *Photo courtesy Kermit Kitts.*

After Church at Oakwood Baptist Church.
Barton Phelps and Virgil Kitts in front of the
church, circa 1940s or 1950s. *Photo courtesy
Kermit Kitts.*

After Church at Oakwood Baptist Church. A
group of men gather outside Oakwood Baptist
Church, 1960s. Rex Roach, J.D. Allen, Ted Lindsey
Jr., and Jack Bond. *Photo courtesy Kermit Kitts.*

Young Women of Emerald Avenue Church. Gladys Kidwell and Nelle Huffaker are the first two ladies on the second row of this picture taken on the front steps of the Huffaker home on Melbourne Street. *Photo courtesy Harold Huffaker.*

Emerald Avenue Methodist Church Board Members. Emerald Avenue Methodist Church board members early 1950's. Note that only two women are on the official board of the church at the time. These two, Eulah Gibbs and Lula Acuff were probably the Communion Steward and the Recording Steward. *Photo courtesy Marsha Robbins.*

Emerald Avenue Methodist Church Special Occasion. Members of Emerald Avenue Methodist Church pose for this formal portrait in the early 1950's. *Photo courtesy Marsha Robbins.*

Emerald Avenue Methodist Youth. Biddy Leahy and Frances Bagwell, 1934 members of the Emerald Avenue Methodist Youth Fellowship (MYF), the origin of the very successful nonprofit Emerald Youth Foundation. *Photo courtesy Biddy Leahy.*

Methodist Youth Mission Trip. Norma Kelley leads an Emerald Avenue Methodist church youth mission trip to Pippa Passes, Kentucky in the summer of 1979 as part of an Appalachian Service project. Front row: John Kelley, Norma Kelley, Mary Roath. Second row: Mike Roberts, Trina Miller, Greg Roath. Third row: Steve Robbin, Randy Moore. *Photo courtesy Norma and Paul Kelley.*

All Dressed Up for Easter. All dressed up for Easter, 1949. The Barlow girls, Wanda, Frances, Joyce and Sue are dressed in their Sunday finest with Easter corsages. *Photo courtesy Sue Newman.*

Three Generations at Lincoln Park Methodist. Back row: Ted Mitchell, Herman Mitchell, Wanda Mitchell, and Carolyn Mitchell who married Vernon Hamilton. Front row: Bryan Mitchell, Janet Hamilton, Karen Hamilton and Ann Mitchell (Snelson). *Photo courtesy Ted Mitchell.*

Mother's Day, May 8, 1960. Mother's Day, May 8, 1960 at Lincoln Park Methodist Church. Back row: John Henegar, and Herman Mitchell. Front row, Leslie Henegar, Dot Mitchell holding Bryan Mitchell, Ted Mitchell, holding baby Ann Mitchell (Snelson) and Wanda Mitchell. *Photo courtesy Ted Mitchell.*

Kids from Emerald Avenue Methodist Church, 1940. Included in this group are Jim Huff, Betty Jo Fisher, Carolyn Moyers, Marsha Cox, Kylene Moyers, Bobbie Witt, and one of the Epps children. *Photo courtesy Marsha Robbins.*

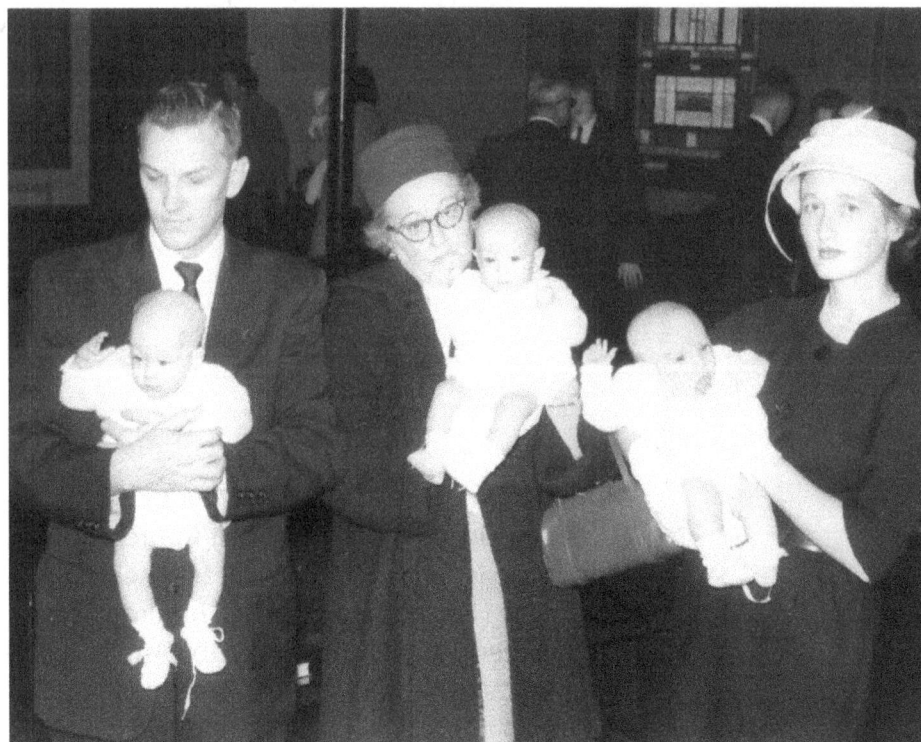

Baptism of Amy, Kelly, and Scotty Bailes, July 28, 1959. With proud parents Bob and Barbara (Gilmer) Bailes at Lincoln Park Methodist Church. *Photo courtesy Barbara and Bob Bailes.*

McMillan Chapel. Members of the Epworth League assembled in front of McMillan Chapel in this 1920s photo. McMillan Chapel was the forerunner church of Emerald Avenue Methodist Church. Front row: Raymond Wood, Willie Mynatt Gibbs, Leonard Parsons, Etta Overton, and Roy Reese, who became prominent in the Holston Methodist Conference. Second row: unknown, Ben Davis, Selah Fisher, Mary Frances Walters. *Photo courtesy Ted Mitchell.*

Sixth Grade from Oakwood School. The 6th grade class of Oakwood Elementary School, 1946 at Emerald Avenue Methodist Church. *Photo courtesy Vernon Hamilton.*

A Baptist Wedding in Lincoln Park. The wedding of Elizabeth "Lib" Peters and James McCluskey at the family home at 335 Springdale Avenue, behind Oakwood Methodist Church. James McCluskey was an early pastor of Wallace Memorial Baptist Church on Merchants Drive, and the couple married while at school at Carson Newman College in the 1950s. Among the guests are Norma, Ethel and Roy Sawyer, Mildred Peters Allen, Bobbie Lindsey, Roy Dobyns, Kay Dobyns, and J. Fred Peters. *Photo courtesy Lib Peters McCluskey.*

Promoting the Neighborhood. A church bulletin from Oakwood Methodist Church from 1937, promoting neighborhood businesses. Note the references to the suburbs of Oakwood and Linwood. Linwood was the area east of Central, just below Sharp's Ridge, south of the CB Atkin Company and just north of Oakwood and west of Lincoln Park. *Photos courtesy Mary Solomon.*

The Wallers. Sophia Waller Love, Ada Waller Bayless, Annie Waller Davis, George M. Waller, and Mac Waller in the yard at 1820 North Central, on the southeast corner of Central at Churchwell Avenue. *Photo courtesy Harold Elkins.*

Sittin' and Standin' Around

There is nothing better than spending a lazy, Sunday afternoon with family and friends around the porch, or in the backyard. The following collection of images are entirely personal, and yet they illustrate well the lives of many families in Oakwood and Lincoln Park. While not historic in the sense of representing a building or a military hero, they are equally historic in documenting life in this community during much of the early 20th century.

These images are now preserved, just as current and future generations need to preserve their own images in this era of the digital and the disposable. Candid moments are often taken for granted, but they should be celebrated and remembered. Today, it's easier than ever to make sure you have a camera around.

The only hard part is remembering to use it, even when it is a part of your cell phone.

Mark Scotty Amy Kelly Robby

Christmas With the Triplets. Mark and Robbie Bailes far left and far right enjoy their first Christmas with their three new siblings, Scotty, Amy and Kelly. Proud parents Bob and Barbara Bailes had the triplets in 1959. *Photo courtesy Barbara and Bob Bailes.*

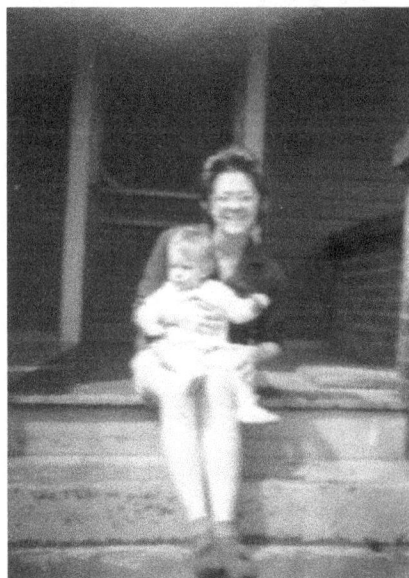

Barbara Asbury. Barbara Asbury, near left, holds her one year old daughter Beth Hutchinson McDonald in front of Jim and Louise Asbury's house at 923 Maynard Avenue. *Photo courtesy Barbara Asbury.*

Pop Hassell. William Hassell , left, holds his son Carroll Holmes Hassell in front of 309 Burwell Avenue. *Photo courtesy Jennifer Montgomery.*

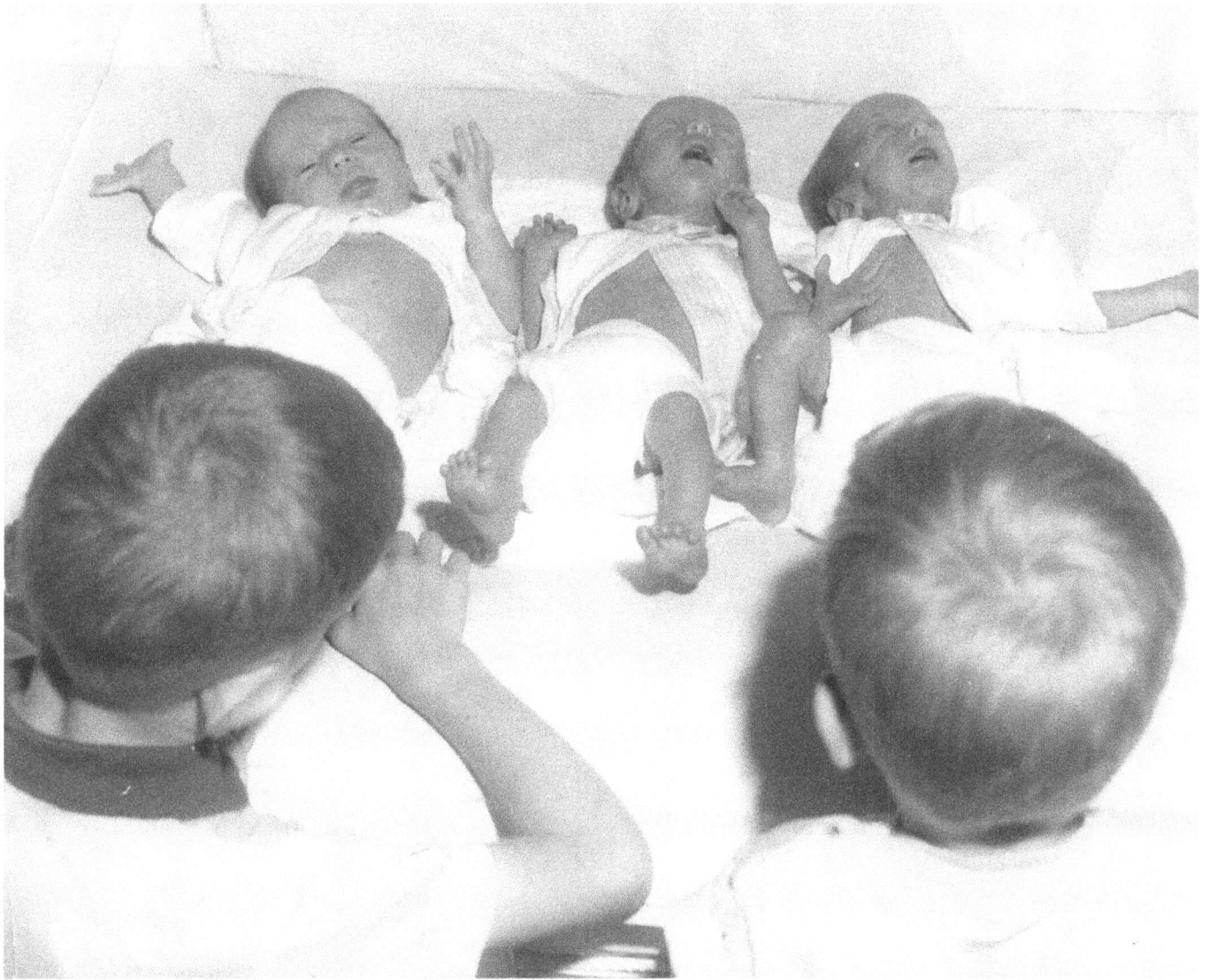

Talk of the Town. Scotty, Amy and Kelly Bailes were the talk of Oakwood and Lincoln Park when they were born at St. Mary's Hospital on Oak Hill Avenue in 1959. *Photo courtesy Barbara and Bob Bailes.*

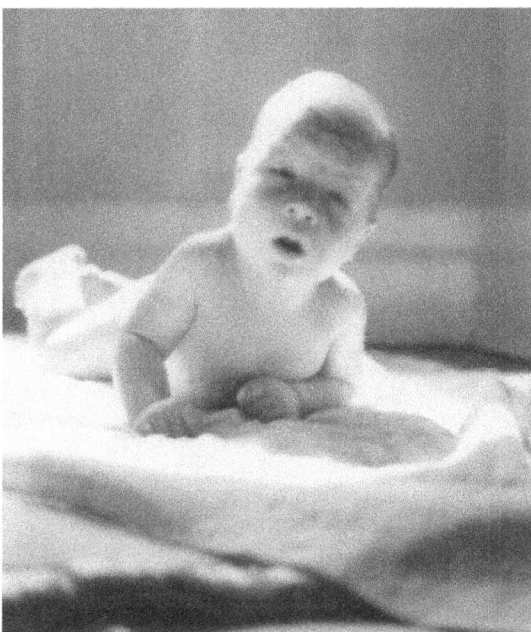

Carroll Hassell. One year old Carroll Hassell, in the front bedroom on Springdale Avenue. *Photo courtesy Jennifer Montgomery.*

Harold Elkins. Harold Elkins celebrates his first birthday on Atlantic Avenue. *Photo courtesy Harold Elkins.*

Ada Bridges. Ada Bridges cares for her flower garden on the side of their large brick home at the corner of North Central and Atlantic Avenue. *Photo courtesy Doris Bridges.*

Ada Bridges. Ada Bridges with her hat on, which many women in early Oakwood and Lincoln Park would wear. *Photo courtesy Doris Bridges.*

Ada Bridges. Another picture of Ada Bridges and her many flowers. *Photo courtesy Doris Bridges.*

Hassell Cousins. At left: Maude Marshall, Mrs. Thomas, Ora Hassell, Charles Marshall, Carroll Hassell, and William Hassell. *Photo courtesy Jennifer Montgomery.*

William and Ora Hassell. William and Ora Hassell, right, pose in front of a springhouse in Lincoln Park circa 1913. William Hassell was a stonecutter on Central Avenue. *Photo courtesy Jennifer Montgomery.*

The Hot Tamale Lady. Lillian Barlow, left, in front of her home at Oldham or Woodland Avenue. Lillian was known as the hot tamale lady of North Knoxville. *Photo courtesy Sue Newman.*

The Cox Family. Larry, Brenda, Shane and Brooke Cox, in front of Emerald Avenue Methodist Church, 1986. *Photo courtesy Larry Cox.*

Clarence Cox. Clarence Cox poses in the snow with children Larry and Marsha Cox (Robbins). *Photo courtesy Larry Cox.*

The Coxes and the McCartts. From left: Avanell McCartt Robinson, Barbara McCartt Owens, Marsha Cox Robbins, Sallie Cox, Eloise McCartt Stephens, William N. Cox, and George Cox, on East Caldwell. Fire Station No. 8 is visible in the background. *Photo courtesy Larry Cox.*

Shopping on Gay Street. Ora Hassell and a friend are caught by a street photographer while shopping on Gay Street. *Photo courtesy Jennifer Montgomery.*

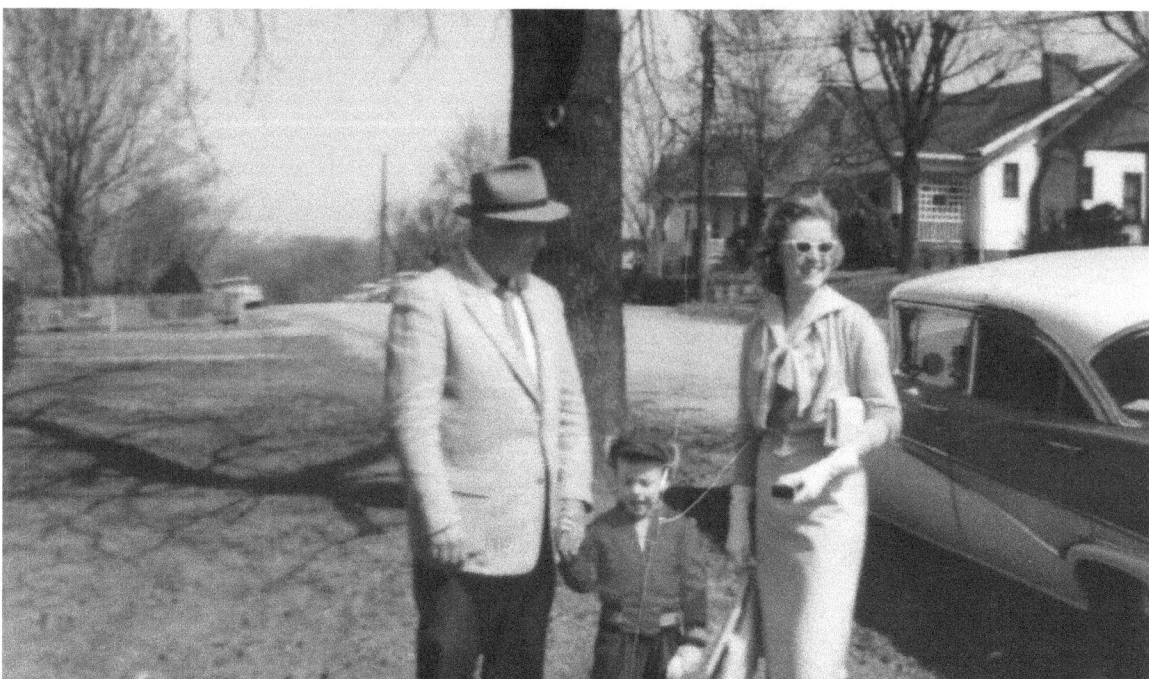

Home from Church. Barbara Asbury with her kid brother Stewart born 1954 and their father Jim Asbury after church coming home to Maynard Avenue. *Photo courtesy Barbara Asbury.*

Walter Barlow. Walter Barlow, who lived on Oldham Avenue, is on the way to work with his lunch pail at Standard Knitting Mills. People said they could set their watch by what time he walked to work. *Photo courtesy Sue Newman.*

Ora Hassell. Ora Hassell in Lincoln Park circa 1920's. *Photo courtesy Jennifer Montgomery.*

Three Amigos. Three good friends from Lincoln Park, left to right Dr. Aubrey Branson, who grew up on Banks Avenue, recovered from polio and went on to become part owner of Park West Hospital; Eual Proffitt who grew up on Atlantic Avenue and owned the grocery store, Proffitt and Branson with Aubrey, Bob Bailes, who was born at 733 Chicamauga, a two story house that is still there. Photo taken 1941. The family also lived on Watauga, Atlantic and Huron. There were a lot of renters in Oakwood and Lincoln Park, but Bob gave his parents the money to buy their house when he came home from the army afer World War II. *Photo courtesy Barbara and Bob Bailes.*

Christmas Party. Christmas party at Dot and Sam Cook's house at 130 Caldwell Avenue. The house is still standing. Dot hosted the party for the Sodaliton Class of Oakwood Baptist Church. Sam owned Sam Cook Service Station at Central and Springdale. Oakwood residents in the picture include Mrs. Chester Sanders, Mrs. Elgie Cox, Katie Reed, Dot Cook, Mrs. Thomas, Elsie Clevenger, Thelma Miller, Jane Kerr, Mrs. Kitts, Mrs. Taylor, and Mrs. Ivester. *Photo courtesy Katherine Cook Thomas.*

Tending Flowers. Grace Ousley tends her garden in their house on Raleigh Avenue. *Photo courtesy Jennifer Montgomery.*

Street Photographer. Mrs. J. Fred Peters and daughters Elizabeth and Mildred are captured by a street photographer on Gay Street in the 1940's. The Peters lived at 335 Springdale and J. Fred Peters owned J. Fred Peters Drygoods, a general work clothes store on Market Square. *Photo courtesy Lib McCluskey Peters.*

John Reece Bayless. John Reece Bayless in front of his home at 354 Atlantic Avenue. *Photo courtesy Harold Elkins.*

Saying Goodbye at the Southern Railway Terminal. Grace and Becky Hassell say goodbye to Paul Hassell, the day he left for the Army in 1942 from the Southern Railway Terminal on Depot Street. *Photo courtesy Jennifer Montgomery.*

Backyard Neighbors. Calvin Neuenschwander and Walter Huffaker enjoy the long shadows of a late summer afternoon in Walter's back yard on Melbourne Street in Oakwood. *Photo courtesy Harold Huffaker.*

Anderson Henderson Stephens. Anderson Henderson Stephens lived with his family at 605 Hiawassee Avenue. A long-time postal clerk, Stephens previously taught in elementary and high schools in Monroe County, where he was born and raised. Among his former students from Monroe County were famed Knoxville lawyer Ray Jenkins, "the Terror of Tellico Plains," as Jenkins was described in his biography, and the late Senator Estes Kefauver. Stephens was a machine gunner overseas during World War I. *Photo courtesy Mary Helen Stephens Kirby.*

Porch Sitting. Annie Gilmer, Mrs. Mitchell and Ida Davis, Annie's sister enjoy an afternoon on the front porch in the 1940's. *Photo courtesy Johnny McReynolds.*

Four Generations. Marsha Robbins, Mrs. B. C. Gibbs, Mrs. Clarence Cox (Willie Mynatt Gibbs) and Baby Jan Robbins Huffaker. Willie and Clarence Cox are the parents of former Knoxville City Councilman Larry Cox and his sister, Marsha Cox Robbins. *Photo courtesy Marsha Robbins.*

Lane Family. Front row: Denny Anderson, Lonnie Roberts, Fran Drinnen. Second row: Carolyn Lane, Gayle Anderson, Retta Anderson, Johnny Mcreynolds, Edna Davenport with baby Larry, Shorty Capps, Jeanny Montgomery, Marcell Drinnen, Dot Lane, Sandy Lane. Third Row: Dewitt Roberts, Howard "Kayo" Montgomery, Hurtle Drinnen, Clyde Anderson, Will Lane, Ollie Lane, Harvey Lane, Alvin Davenport, Bug Lane, Marion Lane holding Bucky. *Photo courtesy Johnny McReynolds.*

The Catheys. Joe and Leona Cathey bought their home at 715 Atlantic Avenue in 1958. Here, Joe proudly displays his car in this 1959 scene. *Photo courtesy Donnie Cathey.*

Chair Tippin'. Loda Belle Barlow Moyers and Hezikiah Berry Moyers enjoy Sunday after lunch tipping chairs in the backyard of their home on Emerald Avenue in this 1940 photograph. *Photo courtesy Sue Newman.*

Neighbors on Woodland Avenue. Walter Barlow, Elsie Barlow Lay, Loda Belle Barlow and George Washington Barlow lived on Woodland Avenue in the 1920's. *Photo courtesy Sue Newman.*

Dogwood Arts Flower Site. Bertie Leek of Ashwood Place takes in the beautiful flowers at the Dogwood Arts camera site at Stevens Mortuary on Oglewood Avenue. *Photo courtesy Emma Jean Leek Huddleston.*

Muz and Maus. Mother and daughter, "Muz" and "Maus." Mary Elizabeth Rutledge and Loda Bell Rutledge take a winter stroll in this 1940 photo on Oldham Avenue. They affectionately referred to themselves as Muz and Maus. *Photo courtesy Sue Newman.*

Bus Reagan. Charles E. "Bus" Reagan, 1904-1980, stands in front of his house 2314 North Central Street. He married Thelma Shields Reagan and operated C. E. Reagan store at 2400 North Central. *Photo courtesy Fletcher Reagan.*

Ollie Mae's First Car. Harold Elkins carefully backs out his mother's first car, a 1952 Ford Mainliner. She had just learned to drive, and never particularly cared for backing up. *Photo courtesy Harold Elkins.*

Mother and Son. Ora Hassell cuddles her younger son Carroll in this circa 1917 photograph on Springdale Avenue. *Photo courtesy Jennifer Montgomery.*

Ruby Davis. Ruby Davis enjoys sitting in the platform rocker at her friend Ada Bayless' home. Ada paid $75 for the rocker. Harold Elkins always remembered the Philco radio. It had a glowing green eye. *Photo courtesy Harold Elkins.*

Harold Elkins Birthday. Harold Elkins birthday, early 1940s on Atlantic Avenue. The tall boy at right is Bud Love. *Photo courtesy Harold Elkins.*

The Hamiltons. Homer Hamilton and his wife Cora pose for this Easter photograph with their children, Dora Lee, Ralph and (in front) Vernon Hamilton on Burwell Avenue in this 1930's photograph. *Photo courtesy Vernon Hamilton.*

The Gilmers. Sam and Annie Gilmer stand on the porch of their home at 520 Chicamauga Avenue across from Lincoln Park School. This home is reported to be one of the first houses built in Lincoln Park. Note a third figure on the right side of the porch who appears to float semi-transparently in front of the clapboard siding on the wall of the porch. If it were a double exposure, how come the siding lines up perfectly? This photograph was taken in 1910 about the year Ruth Gilmer was born. *Photo courtesy Ruth Ann Rogers and Ann Watson.*

At Home in Oakwood-Lincoln Park

From the family dinner table to the front porch, the homes in both Lincoln Park and Oakwood vary greatly, from Victorian cottages to craftsman bungalows, to modest, post-war ranch homes. It is this very diversity that gives Oakwood-Lincoln Park so much of its character. In the following pages, we've gathered a series of images that hopefully illustrate life at home in Oakwood-Lincoln Park, while also showcasing the architectural heritage of the area. Over the years, many homes have received room additions, porches have been expanded or enlarged. More and more individuals and young families recognize the value of homes in the area, and become new neighbors willing to put the blood, sweat, and tears necessary to renovate one of these fine homes.

Home is where the heart is, and for many residents of Oakwood-Lincoln Park, their hearts will always remember the family gatherings, dinners around the table, holidays, birthdays, christenings, graduations, or a receiving of friends after the passing of a loved one. This is indeed home.

Supper Time. Stewart Asbury, and Vesta Sweeting, Charles Sweeting, and Louise Asbury gather around the kitchen table at 923 Maynard Avenue. *Photo courtesy Barbara Asbury.*

Time for Dessert. Doris Asbury Luening, Louise Asbury and Barbara Asbury prepare for dessert around the dining room table in this 1950's photo. *Photo courtesy Barbara Asbury.*

Backyard Dining. The William and Ora Hassell family would frequently enjoy a meal in the back yard of the Hassell home on Springdale Avenue. No deck or patio required even after "Pop" Hassell required the use of a wheelchair. *Photo courtesy Jennifer Montgomery.*

Dinnertime at the Waller Home on Central. From left: Sophia Waller Love, Ollie Mae Martha Waller, George Shields Waller, Annie Waller Davis and Ada Waller Bayless enjoy dinner at the Waller home at 1820 North Central. *Photo courtesy Harold Elkins.*

1950s Kitchen. Another meal in the Waller home. While many homes in Oakwood-Lincoln Park may be modest, they are well suited for large family meals at home. *Photo courtesy Harold Elkins.*

The Ziegler Home. Trula and Doris Bridges standing in the Bridges' family yard on North Central. The home of their friend Katie Ziegler is pictured in the background across the street beside Bridges Grocery. The Ziegler home, according to Doris Bridges, was built "before there were cars." The front of the home featured a porte cochere, open to drive their carriage through, and was probably one of the finest homes built in the 1890s in the Lincoln Park section. *Photo courtesy Doris Bridges.*

Albert and Ada Bridges Home. Albert and Ada Bridges built this beautiful brick home at the corner of North Central and Atlantic Avenue. Before building their home, they rented two other homes in the neighborhood. *Photo courtesy Doris Bridges.*

Mayor James A. Fowler Home, Broadway at Chicamauga. Residence of James A. Fowler, Mayor of Knoxville from 1928-1929. Unidentified girl on sidewalk. The house stood on the corner of Broadway and Chicamauga. It is now the site of Fountain Bowling Lanes behind Senor Taco. Mayor Fowler was part of a delegation of Tennesseeans who went to Washington, D.C. on March 6, 1928 to finalize the terms of the $5 million Rockefeller donation that would secure the creation of the Great Smoky Mountains National Park. *Photo courtesy The Knox County Two Centuries Photograph Project, McClung Historical Collection.*

La Reve. "The Dream," as it was so named on a 1920s postcard of Knoxville, built circa 1910 by building contractor Lynn Hayes and his wife Elizabeth, designed by architect Charles Hayes. The home has been in the Howard family for the last 60 years, and maintains its residential appearance while providing offices for the Howard's pumbing, heating and air business. *Photo courtesy Park City Press.*

A Christmas Photograph at Home. A Christmas photograph at home. Left to right, Ada Bridges, daughters Trula and Doris, and Albert Bridges. The Bridges owned Bridges Grocery at 2730 North Central. *Photo courtesy Doris Bridges.*

168

William and Ollie Rose Lane Home. This modest but handsome home at 534 Cedar was purchased by William Andrew Lane and Ollie Rose Lane in 1923. Ollie lived there until 1979. *Photo courtesy Johnny McReynolds.*

The Blizzard of 1952. Photo of Ada Bayless's home at 354 Atlantic Avenue during the blizzard of 1952, when Knoxville received 18 inches of snow. *Photo courtesy Harold Elkins.*

115 East Oakhill Avenue, Oakwood. Willie Mynatt Gibbs, right, poses with her brother Howard and sister Lallah in front of the family home at 115 East Oakhill Avenue. The site is now the parking lot for BESCO. *Photo courtesy Larry Cox.*

From Victorian to Craftsman. Another view of 520 Chicamauga (see page 163) after the more Craftsman style front porch was added and the trees had matured. *Photo courtesy Ruth Ann Rogers and Ann Watson.*

520 Chicamauga. view of 520 Chicamauga. Note the elaborate swing in the yard. The home is still standing after over 100 years. *Photo courtesy Ruth Ann Rogers and Ann Watson.*

Homer and Cora Hamilton's Home. Homer and Cora Hamilton's house at 319 Burwell. *Photo courtesy Vernon Hamilton.*

Applewood. Every home should have a name. What was originally the Asbury home at 923 Maynard Avenue has been lovingly restored by Mr. Lee Bailey and is known today as Applewood. *Photo courtesy Barbara Asbury.*

A 1950s View of Applewood. The shiny chrome on this Asbury family car stands in stark contrast to the quiet, humble nature of this Craftsman bungalow. *Photo courtesy Barbara Asbury.*

Hassell Home, 416 Springdale Avenue. The Ora and William Hassell home at 416 Springdale in this damaged 100-year-old photo from 1910. *Photo courtesy Jennifer Montgomery.*

Room Additions Were Common. Ada Waller Bayless took this photo of her home at 354 Atlantic Avenue after she added two new rooms on the back, and got a new roof and porch. *Photo courtesy Harold Elkins.*

From Streetcar to Pontiac. The Cathey family proudly displays a fleet of 1955 Pontiacs in front of their home at 715 Atlantic Avenue. After the end of street car service to Oakwood and Lincoln Park in 1947, the neighborhood witnessed the rise of the automobile. *Photo courtesy Donnie Cathey.*

800 Silver Dollars. John Reece Bayless and Ada Waller Bayless bought their home at 354 Atlantic Avenue in 1938 with 800 silver dollars that Ada had meticulously saved. *Photo courtesy Harold Elkins.*

Cox Home, 1015 Emerald Avenue. The home of Clarence and Willie Cox at 1015 Emerald Avenue. Their kids being former Councilman Larry Cox and Marsha Cox Robbins. *Photo courtesy Larry Cox.*

Atlantic Avenue. Home on Atlantic Avenue, opposite 354 Atlantic. *Photo courtesy Harold Elkins.*

Hassell Home, Burwell Avenue. William Hassell (in wheelchair), Ora Hassell at back on right, circa 1930s-1940s, on Burwell Avenue. *Photo courtesy Jennifer Montgomery.*

Hassell Home, 416 Springdale Avenue. Ora Hassell holds the small hand of her son Carroll, at home on Springdale Avenue. *Photo courtesy Jennifer Montgomery.*

Cedar Avenue, circa 1929. 1929 photograph in the 300 block of Cedar Avenue. Left to right: Lyda Davis, Ruby Davis, Ollie Mae Bayless Elkins, Sylvan Love, Jimmy Davis, Clarence Love. The home in the background belongs to James Davis. *Photo courtesy Harold Elkins.*

The Underwoods. A photo of Edgar and Ethel Underwood and their two sons, possibly at 332 Oak Hill Avenue in Oakwood. Edgar, the nephew of Mayor Rufus Underwood and Emma Herrell Underwood was officer in the United States Navy. He married Ethel Mize from Lincoln Park. *Photo courtesy Edna Mae Frances Scarborough.*

Springdale Avenue. T.L. Hamm, Dora Lee Hamilton Hamm, Helen Walker, Leonard Walker, Mamie Walker, Cora Hamilton and Homer Hamilton pose for this photograph on Springdale Avenue. *Photo courtesy Vernon Hamilton.*

Cathey Home, Atlantic Avenue. The home of Joe and Leona Cathey at 715 Atlantic Avenue. They purchased this home in 1958. *Photo courtesy Donnie Cathey.*

New Home. The Laugherty family move into their new home at 702 Churchwell Avenue in 1941. *Photo courtesy Mary Jean Laugherty Larison and Carolyn Laugherty Overton.*

Pony ride. Mark Scarborough Jr. and his sister Edna Mae take pony ride in front of the family home on 221 East Quincy Avenue circa 1920. Their father Mark (Marcus) A. Scarborough Sr. was a payroll clerk at Brookside Mills. He married Loe Keisling December 20, 1911. Loe Keisling Scarborough worked in the President's office at Emory and Henry College in Virginia. *Photo courtesy Edna Mae Frances Scarborough.*

Child's Play

Make no mistake, children will always find time to play. Whether Mom and Dad buy a fine birthday gift or the kids create a castle from an empty refrigerator box, our imagination as children is pretty infinite.

Some of the best images of life in Oakwood-Lincoln Park are seen through the eyes of children, whether it is as they learn to ride a tricycle nearly 100 years ago, or riding a pony through the neighborhood. From modest birthday celebrations to playing in the snow, these scenes are gifts today to those who remember a simpler time, and gifts too, to young families today who simply need to breathe and remember how much fund it is to turn off the electronics and take the kids outside for a simple game.

Sometimes it is as simple as playing with the dog. Sometimes it is a grand scouting adventure, just playing in the dirt, or receiving a cherished gift at Christmas. How many of us remember that first bicycle, or how hard our parents worked to balance the Christmas gifts among the children and not let us realize just how tight the family budget was? These are realities not only of a generation past, but are instructive to a new generation of parents. It is not about the stuff. It is about the joy.

Shorty and Bug. Shorty and Bug. Elva "Shorty" Lane and William Earl "Bug" Lane goof around in Depression era Lincoln Park. Lincoln Park Methodist Church is faintly visible in the background of this damaged image. William Andrew Lane and Ollie Rose Lane bought their house at 534 Cedar in 1923. *Photo courtesy Johnny McReynolds.*

Remember When We Used to Get Snow? A blizzard covers little Donnie Cathey and the family car at 715 Atlantic Avenue, early 1960's. Right: A wider angle shows the streetscape of tidy houses enveloped in snow on Atlantic Avenue. *Photo courtesy Donnie Cathey.*

Birthday Party! Larry Cox celebrates his birthday at home at 1015 East Emerald Avenue next to Fulton High School with friends from the neighborhood. *Photo courtesy Larry Cox.*

Larry and Marsha Cox. Larry and Marsha Cox enjoy a fun afternoon with the family dogs. *Photo courtesy Larry Cox.*

Back from Fishing. Mrs. Sally Cox and her husband Arthur prepare to cook up a mess of fish after a family outing with little Larry Cox. *Photo courtesy Larry Cox.*

Maude Marshall and Carroll Hassell. Maude Marshall helps her second cousin Carroll Hassell learn the finer points of riding his tricycle on Springdale Avenue in the early 1920's. *Photo courtesy Jennifer Montgomery.*

Away We Go! Carroll Hassell masters the tricycle and pedals away down Springdale Avenue, early 1920s. *Photo courtesy Jennifer Montgomery.*

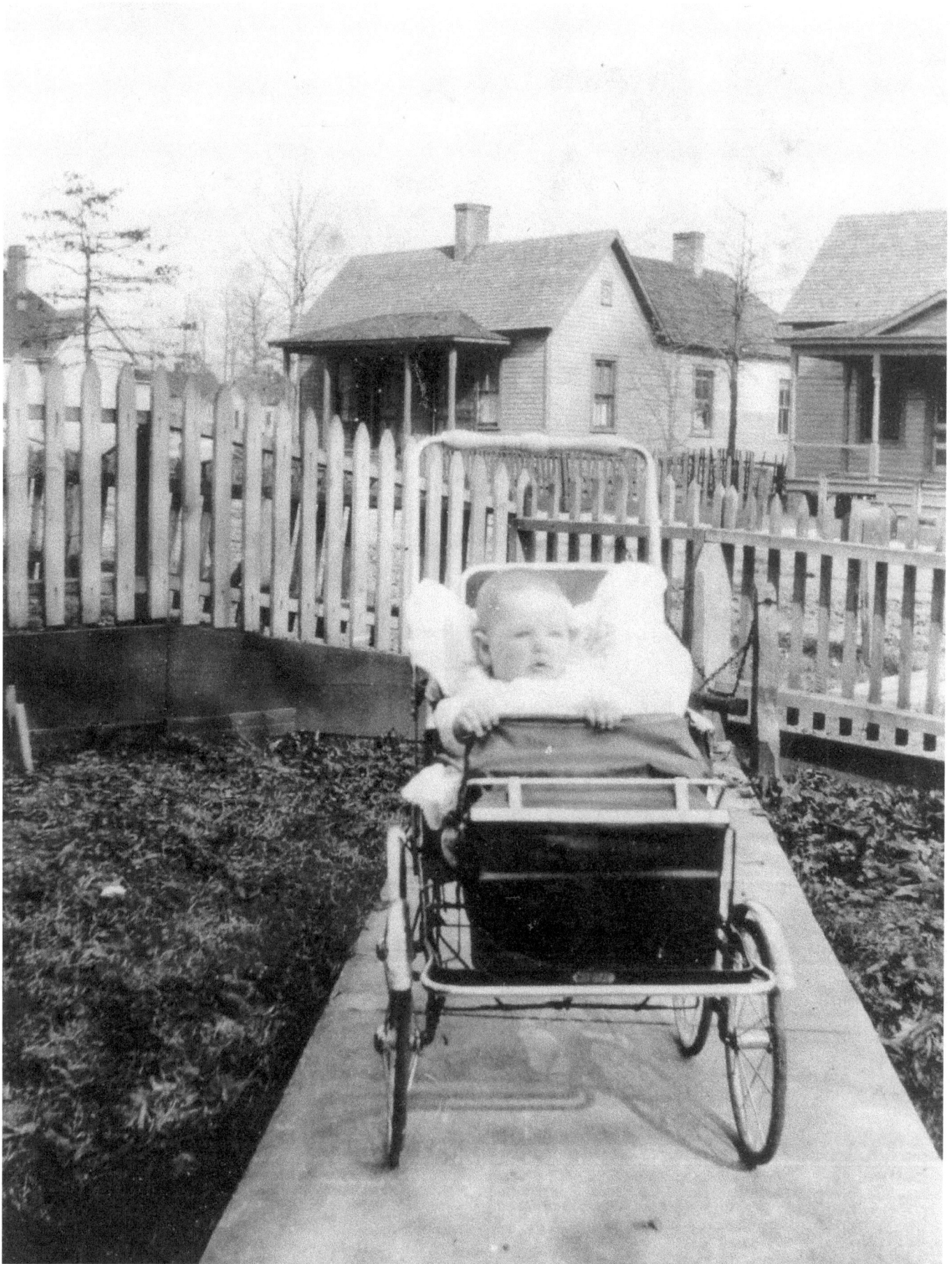

Baby Buggy. Carroll Hassell take a stroll in a very fine baby buggy on Morelia Avenue. Several homes are visible in the background. This angled sidewalk is approximately three blocks east of Central. *Photo courtesy Jennifer Montgomery.*

Don't Get Those Pretty Dresses Dirty. Edna Mae Lane, Johnny Lane (McReynolds), Jeanny Lane Montgomery, Mary Louise James, the daughter of Trigg James, the pastor of Lincoln Park Methodist Church and Marlene Mitchell. Mary Louise was clearly enjoying herself more than the other four girls as she makes a face at the camera. The Lincoln Park Methodist parsonage was located on Cedar. *Photo courtesy Johnny McReynolds.*

How did I Get in This Bowl? Carroll Hassell is clearly unhappy with bath time on the front porch on Springdale Avenue. *Photo courtesy Jennifer Montgomery.*

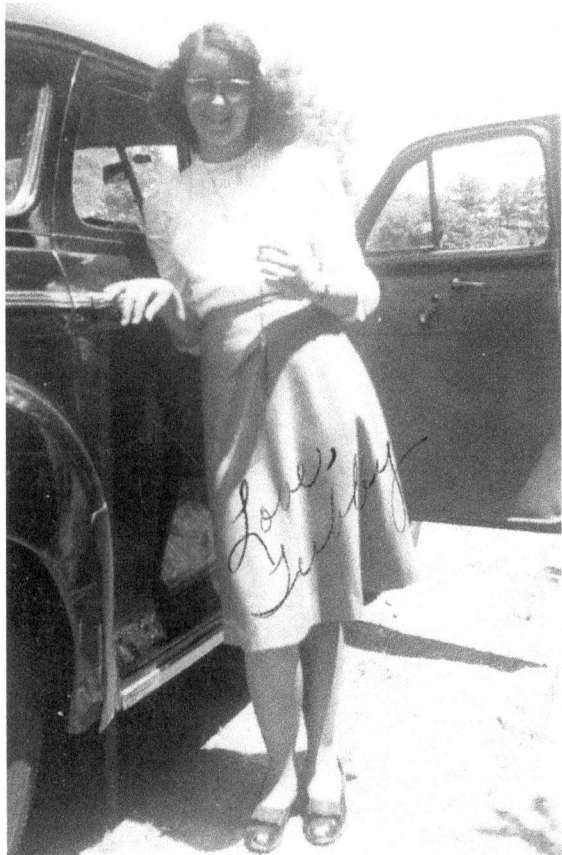

A Dog Named Sing. Left: Harvey Lane plays with his beautiful black chow named Sing at the family home on Cedar Street. Right: Carolyn "Tubby" Mitchell mugs for the camera in this 1940's photograph. *Photo courtesy Johnny McReynolds, Katherine Cook Thomas.*

Dogs and Cats. Left: A much older Carroll Hassell gets a performance out of his dog Boots at home on Raleigh Avenue. Right: Grady Spaulding and his daughter Evelyn regard a new litter of kittens with an unknown friend circa 1929 to 1934. Evelyn would marry Walter Amman Jr. *Photos courtesy Jennifer Montgomery, left, and Grady Amman, right.*

186

Boy Scout Troop 49. Boy Scout Troop 49 in the early 1960s with Scoutmaster Harold Huffaker. Huffaker started the troop in 1955. Helping through the years were such good men as John Reese, Dr. Ellis Hunt, Bill Puryear, Gordon Patterson, Mike Moyers, Don Longmire, Tip Barnes, Tom Addington, Paul McBee, Fred Kyles, Dr. Lea Acuff, Doug Harris, Quinton Alexander, Mr. Taylor, Mike Leahy, Bill Banks, Charles Banks, Casey Routh, Gene Routh, Len Harris, Ted Bowles, Mr. Carmichael, Mr. Bridgeman, Dr. Sonny Evans, Paul Lee, Ivan Lusk, Bill Spangler, Bob Oliver, Ben Barbee, and Paul Kelley. Some of the boys only had one parent, and Troop 49 became an important part of many young men's lives during the 38 years from 1955 until 1993, when David Bost became scoutmaster. *Photo courtesy Harold Huffaker.*

The Oakwood Boys. The Oakwood boys. Scoutmaster Harold Huffaker took Boy Scout Troop 49 on a 50 mile hike in this August 1976 image. All of the boys in the picture are from Oakwood. Left to right: Michael Kelley, Randy Moore, Steve Robbins. *Photo courtesy Harold Huffaker.*

Uncle Stewart. Young Stewart Asbury plays with his little niece Beth on a beautiful spring day on Maynard Avenue. Right: Barbara Asbury and her little brother Stewart in the garden on Maynard Avenue. *Photo courtesy Barbara Asbury.*

Gotta Love Dirt. Carroll Hassell plays in a big pile of sand. Note the homes in the background on Springdale Avenue. *Photo courtesy Jennifer Montgomery.*

In the Yard. James Lee and Cyndy Bailes at the Lee house on Morelia Avenue. *Photo courtesy Cyndy Cox.*

Pedal Car. A young Dora Lee Hamilton scoots her pedal car down Burwell Avenue circa 1920s. *Photo courtesy Vernon Hamilton.*

Camp Mary Ijams. Bobbie Sawyer, Norma Kelley's sister works hard with three other girls at Camp Mary Ijams Girl Scout Camp in South Knoxville in 1945. *Photo courtesy Norma and Paul Kelley.*

Certificate of Membership. Ethel Sawyer, mother of Bobbie and Norma Sawyer proudly served as a committee member of Girl Scout troop #7 as evidenced by this certificate of membership. Alice Heap, a Knoxville City Schools teacher, was the long-time leader of Troop #7, to which many Lincoln Park girls belonged. *Photo courtesy Norma and Paul Kelley.*

Girl Scout Troop #179, late 1950s. Center, Judy Bayless. Left to right: Judy Bridgeman, Peggy Peterson, Kae Jarmon, Faye Kraph, Mary Johnson, Betty Crawford, Janice Jones, Elizabeth Keesee, Dinah Roberts. These two images were taken on the steps inside the Christenberry Club House. *Photo courtesy Emma Jean Leek Huddleston.*

Girl Scout Troop #179. First met at Christenberry Junior High School. First row: Mrs. Blackburn, Elizabeth Keesee, Dinah Roberts, Judy Bayless, Ms. Johnson, Emma Jean Leek. Second row: Judy Bridgman, Janice Jones, Carolyn Andes, Linda Sue Dickenson. Third row: Kae Jarmon, Peggy Peterson, Betty Crawford, Faye Kraph. Fourth row: Sue Cook, Margretta Cameron. *Photo courtesy Emma Jean Leek Huddleston.*

Christmas 1953. Doris and Harold Elkins, Christmas 1953. *Photo courtesy Harold Elkins.*

Pam French's Birthday Party. Pam French, daughter of Ed and Tenneva French, enjoys her birthday party on Atlantic Avenue with all of her young friends. *Photo courtesy Harold Elkins.*

Bathing Beauties. Bathing beauties in Oakwood. Left to right: Bobbie Lindsey, Betty Faye Henry, Mary Dodson, and Nancy Buckner. *Photo courtesy Kermit Kitts.*

Rowdy Girls. The rowdy girls of Lincoln Park. Such cute grins on the faces of these girls in the back yard of 530 Cedar Street circa 1933. The house is till standing. Front row: Johnny Lane and Jeanette Hall. Back row: Jeanny Lane Montgomery, Joanna, Mary Hall, and Edna Mae Lane. *Photo courtesy Johnny McReynolds.*

Snow White and Rose Red. Nancy Buckner and her mother Polly enjoy the story of Snow White and Rose Red. The Buckners lived on East Columbia Avenue. Nancy married Kermit Kitts. *Photo courtesy Kermit Kitts.*

Western Flyer. Doris and Harold Elkins show off their new bicycles their parents purchased at the Western Auto in Happy Holler on Central, mid 1950s. Harold sports a Western Flyer, while Doris' bicycle is a Shelby. *Photo courtesy Harold Elkins.*

Boys on Central. Kermit Kitts and his younger brother Gordon in front of the Kitts home in the 2600 block of North Central. Many fine homes once stood on Central. *Photo courtesy Kermit Kitts.*

Children of the Manhattan Project in Lincoln Park. The yard of Grandma Annie Gilmer's house at 520 Chicamauga across the street from Lincoln Park School was transformed in the early 1940's when 20 small trailers were set up in the yard for Oak Ridge workers during the Manhattan project. Here young Ruth Ann and Bill Leake play with some of the children of the Oak Ridge workers on Grandma Gilmer's yard swing. Note the size of the trailer in the background. *Photo courtesy Ruth Ann Rogers, Ann Watson.*

Boys at Play. Stewart Asbury, J.R. Ridenour, J.R.'s sister, and Chuck Stevens at play near Maynard Avenue in the 1950's. *Photo courtesy Barbara Asbury.*

Hand Operated See-Saw. A dutiful Louis Hassell plays with his younger brother Carroll in this photo from the late 1910s. Note the creative see saw, apparently hand-operated with a handle. Louis died in a tragic boy scout accident at Lyons Bend in West Knox County. *Photo courtesy Jennifer Montgomery.*

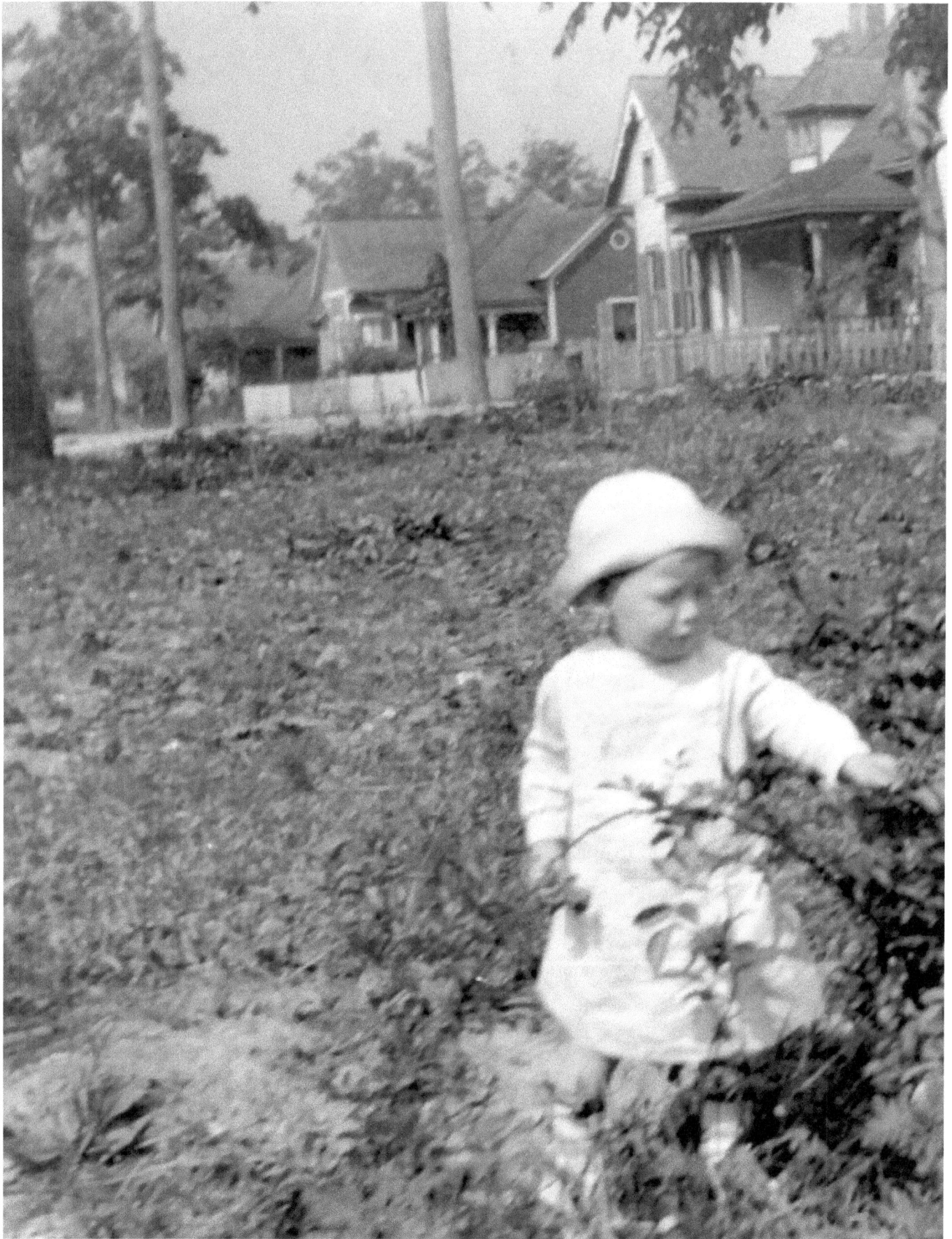

Springdale at Harvey. An adventurous young Carroll Hassell plays in some brambles near at Springdale Avenue near Harvey Street circa 1915. Note the homes in the background. *Photo courtesy Jennifer Montgomery.*

Pajama Party. Katherine Cook and friends pose on the back steps of Dot and Sam Cook's house at 130 Caldwell Avenue. Katherine was having a pajama party in this 1940's image. Left to right: Joyce Satterfield, Carolyn Mitchell, Jody Plers, Katherine Cook. Front row: Charlie Jean Endy, Carol McIntyre. *Photo courtesy Katherine Cook Thomas.*

Smiling Faces. Becky and Tom Hassell, children of Grace and Paul Hassell. *Photo courtesy Jennifer Montgomery.*

Girls' Softball Champs. The Christenberry Junior High School girls' softball team were 1948 champions in their division in the City Recreation Bureau League. Front row: Sue Donna Burko, right field; Melba Connant, centerfield; Capt. Anne Davis, catcher; Tootsie Howell, second base; and Carole Straine, shortstop. Second row: Norma Sawyer, third base; Carolyn McMillan, left field; Midge Lambdin, sub; and Manager Georigie Harb. Pitcher Betty Lebow and first baseman Julie Harb were absent when the picture was taken. *Photo courtesy Norma and Paul Kelley.*

Champions Never Make Excuses. The Fulton Baby Falcons, 1954 team. Now called the Knoxville Falcons, the community football league is in its 55th season, and has grown from one team to eight, with players from 4 to 14 years old. Coaches in this photo are Coach McDonald and Coach Mike Leahy. The water boy grew up to become Dr. Doug Leahy, son of Biddy and Mike Leahy. Also recognized in this photo are #28, Dick Puryear, #50, Bill Keith, and #21, Coach Bob Black at Fulton High School. a 7th and 8th grade recreation league football team, have been playing in North Knoxville for over 50 years. *Photo courtesy Larry Cox.*

Oakwood Baseball. Front row, left to right: Lloyd Frye, Ernie Roberts, Bill Fretwell, Claude Hammer, Edge Ward. Back row: Clyde Ward, Buck Hammer, Red Hutchison, Charlie Swaggerty, Ham Kitts, Bennie Stephens, Luke Wright. Batboy: Tommy Moreland. *Photo courtesy Kermit Kitts.*

Play Ball. Arthur Clay Stephens suits up to play ball. *Photo courtesy Mary Helen Stephens Kirby.*

Stephens Family. Family of Anderson Henderson Stephens at 605 Hiawassee Avenue. *Photo courtesy Mary Helen Stephens Kirby.*

"To Turn the World." John Kelley, the son of Norma and Paul Kelley wrote the winning song while a student at Fulton High School which became the official song of the 1982 Knoxville World's Fair. *Photo courtesy Norma and Paul Kelley.*

Album Liner. Album liner for the souvenir record "To Turn the World". *Photo courtesy Norma and Paul Kelley.*

The Lincoln Park Boys. This priceless 1930's photo was taken after church at Gilmer's filling station at Pershing and Chicamauga. Two of boys pictured here, Hartsell Bailes and Johnny Lily, would die in the impending World War. Hartsell was killed at Luzon in the Phillipines, and Johnny who joined the Marine Corps the day after Pearl Harbor, was killed at Guadalcanal. Many Lincoln Park and Oakwood boys joined the service right after Pearl Harbor. Some of the boys pictured here include Ray Jennings, Bob and Charles Pennington, Vernon Taylor with the mop of hair, and David Taylor (little boy). Jack Bowman is in the leather jacket in the center and standing far left is Earl "Bug" Lane. Visible in the background, far right is a wall and window of Lincoln Park School. *Photo courtesy Barbara and Bob Bailes.*

In the Service of Their Country

The images and stories in this chapter offer a glimpse of that "greatest generation" of young people who volunteered and answered the call to service during wartime.

This war, beyond all others, affected our nation and our neighborhoods. The effect of this particular war is visible today in its influence on residential architecture, where "post-war" homes in Oakwood and Lincoln Park are clearly distinguishable from "pre-war" homes. From wartime rationing on the homefront to letters and post cards sent, even to one of our own in a German prisoner of war camp, the impact of World War II fell heavily on Oakwood and Lincoln Park. Never forget these humble heroes who bravely served. While most returned home to begin a career in business and raise a family, at least three Oakwood-Lincoln Park boys, including two pictured above, never made it home.

This chapter is for Hartsell Bailes, Johnny Lily, and Jimmy Wallace (see page 210), three young men who made the ultimate sacrifice.

So Proud of His Big Brother. Vernon Hamilton, his older brother Ralph and their father Homer Hamilton on Gay Street during World War II. *Photo courtesy Vernon Hamilton.*

Uncle Jess Walker. Uncle Jess Walker served in the navy during World War I. He died in 1938. *Photo courtesy Vernon Hamilton.*

Wartime Family Portrait. Three of the five Bailes boys who served during World War II are pictured here—Walt, Robert, and Carl "Curly" Bailes. Their two brothers Frank "Red" Bailes and Hartsell Bailes were already overseas. Hartsell was killed in action in the Phillippines. Robert (Bob) did his basic training at Fort McClellan, Alabama after finishing ROTC at Old Knoxville High School. He was on his way to the Pacific for the invasion of Japan when the United States dropped the atomic on Hiroshima, Japan in August, 1945. He ended up on the USS Gordon, a 5000-man troop ship at Inchon, Korea for six months. Seventy six of them were not supposed to be on that ship, but their records were lost and they received no pay. He was there with Ralph Chaney, who played fullback at the University of Tennessee. They lived off their 50-cent cigarette ration, not smoking them, but selling them to the Koreans for $6 a pack. Bob finally made it home in March, 1946 and worked for the telephone company for thirty eight years. Carl became general manager of Chapman Drug. Red returned home and became a beloved sports writer for the Knoxville News Sentinel, and Bob's wife Barbara worked for many years in the office at C.B. Atkin Company in Lincoln Park. *Photo courtesy Barbara and Bob Bailes.*

Jimmy Wallace, Killed in Action at Normandy. The Barlow family poses on the Oglewood Avenue bridge in this early 1940's photo. Their cousin, Jimmy Wallace, far right, was killed during the Normandy invasion in 1944. *Photo courtesy Sue Newman.*

Ed and Tenneva French. Ed French and Tenneva Love French, 1944. Photo *courtesy Harold Elkins.*

Admiral Maurice F. Weisner

Maurice Franklin Weisner grew up at 306 Burwell Avenue in Oakwood, the son of Clint and Adra Weisner. Clint Weisner was a fireman with the Southern Railway. Born November 20, 1917 just as World War I was ending, Maurice "Mick" Weisner grew up in Oakwood, attended the University of Tennessee for two years before transferring to the U.S. Naval Academy. He married Norma Holland Smith, the daughter of Mr. and Mrs. Charles L. Smith. Maurice and Norma attended high school and UT together, and Norma, who passed away in 2005, was a member of UT's class of '41. Weisner served in World War II as a naval aviator aboard the USS *Wasp* (CV-7) until it was sunk in September, 1942. A highly decorated officer in the Navy, Weisner received two Defense Distinguished Service Medals, and two Distinguished Flying Crosses, among many other awards.

Weisner served as commander of the USS *Guadalupe*, the USS *Coral Sea*, the *USS Ranger*, and the USS *Enterprise*. He became a four-star admiral who served as Vice Chief of Naval Operations from 1972-1973, Commander-in-Chief, U.S. Pacific Fleet (CINCPACFLT) from 1973-1976, and Commander in Chief, U.S. Pacific Command (CINCPAC) from 1976-1979.

In his autobiography, *It Doesn't Take a Hero*, General Norman Schwarzkopf describes a meeting in Admiral Weisner's conference room, when Schwarzkopf was a young brigadier general:

> *Pacific Command was situated in the hills west of Honolulu at a Marine base named Camp Smith. The three-story stucco headquarters had been built originally as a hospital and wasn't much to look at. But the setting was spectacular: palm trees, banyan trees, elephant ear plants, mango trees laden with ripe fruit, and lovely tropical flowers in every shade of red imaginable...On my first morning (Jack Sadler) introduced me to my new boss, Rear Admiral Don Shelton, the chief of plans and policy for the command. Next, Sadler led me to a conference room where Admiral Maurice F. Weisner, the commander in chief of Pacific Command and Shelton's boss, was about to start the morning's staff meeting. The room was dominated by a large U-shaped table where Weisner presided, flanked by generals and admirals who headed various sections of the staff...I reassured myself by remembering that, seated at the table or not, I was about to be privy to the inner workings of one of America's most important headquarters. Pacific Command's area of responsibility extended from the west coast of the United States to the east coast of Africa--covering literally almost half of the world. On sea, it spanned the entire Pacific Ocean and the entire Indian Ocean; on land, it was responsible for everything east of the Iran-Pakistan border including India, Indochina, Australia, New Zealand, Indonesia, the Philippines, Japan, and South Korea.*

MAURICE FRANKLIN WEISNER

KNOXVILLE, TENN.

Mick is a Tennessean through and through : he has lived the greatest part of his life in Knoxville.

While he was still called Maurice, his interests turned from the three "r's" to parades, uniforms, and guns. During high school he had four years in the R. O. T. C. He was a student for two years at the University of Tennessee in their Civil Engineering school. There too, he found much time for military, and decided to make a career of it. Then he chose Annapolis over West Point.

His slap on the back and sharp voice are familiar to most of us. He adapts himself well to any situation and makes the best of it ; but he is not without moods. None can be happier, but none can be more gloomy.

Of course he has changed some since we have known him ; he is a little older, a little harder, and a little wiser. Nevertheless, he is a fine gentleman with enough of the deep South in him to be diplomatic. Mickey will do well anywhere.

Boat Club 4, 3, 2, 1 ; Company Representative 3, 2 ; Track 4 ; Battalion Football 4 ; Battalion Boxing 3.

Weisner died October 15, 2006, and is buried at Barrancas National Cemetery in Pensacola, Florida. Upon his passing, U.S. Chief of Naval Operations, Admiral Mike Mullen issued a special message:

"Every man and woman serving our Navy today joins me in mourining the death of retired Adm. Maurice F. Weisner, World War II hero and former commander of the U.S. Pacific Fleet and U.S. Pacific Command. We extend humbly to his family our thoughts, prayers, and deepest sympathies in their time of grief and sorrow. Admiral Weisner served his nation nobly for the better part of four decades. He did so at peace and at war, at sea and ashore all over the world. On his chest they pinned Distinguished Service Medals from the Department of Defense, Army, Air Force and four from the Navy; two awards of the Legion of Merit; two Distinguished Flying Crosses; six Air Medals; a Navy Commendation Medal with Combat "V"; five unit commendations; and a host of campaign and service medals. Foreign decorations from Japan, the Republic of Korea, Republic of Vietnam, Phillippine Republic, Kingdom of Thailand, and the United Nations also grace his uniform.

But it was never about the honors or the medals. For Admiral Weisner, it was about the mission and about his people. He learned that lesson aboard the USS Wasp in September of 1942, when three torpedoes from a Japanese submarine slammed into the ship's side, killing nearly 200 of the crew. And he learned it again just three years later, when flying off the deck of another aircraft carrier, he sank a Japanese destroyer escort. From command of three aircraft squadrons right up through command of all U.S. forces in the Pacific, Admiral Weisner stayed dedicated to the ideal of service and shipmate before self.

As we mourn his passing, so too should we reflect on his contributions to our Navy—of the thousands of lives he guided, the careers he mentored, the difference he made globally by being a strong leader. He ushered in a new era of sea power, helping this nation win the Cold War just as he had helped it win World War II. Indeed, modern naval aviation still stands on his broad shoulders. We would all do well to remember the remarkable legacy of this truly great man."

Maurice F. Weisner, U.S. Naval Academy Yearbook, 1941. Maurice "Mick" Weisner, in the *Lucky Bag*, the yearbook of the U.S. Naval Academy. *Photo courtesy Ancestry.com.*

The Dashing Mike Leahy. The dashing Mike Leahy in desert uniform. Mike served in the United States Army during World War II fighting against Rommel's German forces in North Africa, then continuing into Italy at Enzio. Mike and Biddy Leahy were married in 1945. Friends drove them to Gatlinburg for their honeymoon since they didn't yet have a car. Mike graduated from Old Knoxville in 1939. Biddy said they were so poor they couldn't afford an annual. Another classmate Foster Arnett Sr. wrote what life was like in a yearbook made fifty or sixty years later. *Photo courtesy Biddy Leahy.*

Bug Lane. William Earl "Bug" Lane, 1921-2008, in a 1942 US Navy portrait. A young Marcell Lane tried to call him "brother," but it always came out "Bug." Bug served on the USS Saratoga in the US Navy and was on the ship when it was torpedoed at the Battle of the Coral Sea. Badly listing, the ship limped back to Pearl Harbor. Bug survived and went to work for Betty Crocker before purchasing West Hill Dry Cleaners. *Photo courtesy Johnny McReynolds.*

LOCKHEED P-38 "LIGHTNING"

The crews of these planes "Have The Drop" on everything under the sun, just so long as we keep them aloft. Plane production cannot be maintained unless you buy your share of War Bonds and War Stamps.

Hello Sammie
Here is another
picture of an unusual
plane for you.
I hope your getting
along OK.
Your Pal
Morris
Hope your mother is
feeling better

POST CARD

Mr "Sammie" Bratton
129 E. Emerald
Knoxville, Tennessee

B-17E "FLYING FORTRESS"

Hello SAMMIE
HERE'S YOU ANOTHER
picture of ONE of
OUR GREATEST Planes
This Bomber is doing
A Lot to help US WIN
The WAR.
Well tell Mr. PARMAK
AND MRS. BRATTON Hello
for ME.
Love to all
Morris

Mr Sammie Bratton
129 E. Emerald
Knoxville, Tennessee

Postcards from Bomber School. Morris Epps, the son of Gale Franklin Epps and Mildred Fortune Epps, lived with his Mom and Dad at 316 East Anderson Avenue, a little further south of Oakwood in Happy Holler. The family attended Emerald Avenue Methodist Church. On December 7, 1941, Morris was on a double date down at the intersection of Broadway and Central with his girlfriend from Fountain City, Wanda Johnson, along with Babe Webster and Jim Porter, when they heard the first **(cont. on page 216)**

Lt. Morris F. Epps

Lieutenant Morris Epps served with "The Mighty Eighth" out of Seething, East Anglia, England. On his fifth mission (June 18, 1944) his plane was shot down over Hamburg, Germany. He was captured by the Luftwaffe, taken to Dulag Luft and then to Stalag Luft III where he was placed in the South Compound, Barrack 128, Combine 13. On January 27, 1945, he was in ill health when the South Compound was ordered to lead a forced evacuation of Stalag Luft III. After marching 35 miles in 27 hours, his section rested in a glass factory in Muskau and then departed, leaving the sick behind with the West Compound men. He later moved to a pottery factory, a paper factory, and finally to another pottery factory where he joined the men of Center Compound with whom he completed the fifty-two mile march and the subsequent 72-hour boxcar ride. His journey ended at Stalag VIIA in Moosburg, where he stayed until liberated on April 29, 1945. After liberation, he returned home to his wife in Knoxville, Tennessee. He sought a life of helping others and began a career in education after college, working in Virginia and New Jersey. He dearly loved teaching and spent several years in the classroom. Afterwards, he served in a number of administrative leadership positions, including superintendent of schools.

His daughter, Becky Lawson, who now resides in Michigan, participated in a re-enactment walk of the march in January, 2009.

In 2004, Becky was going through some of her dad's correspondence, she recognized how dedicated Pastor Samuel E. Bratton was to his flock. When her father was take prisoner at Stalag Luft III in 1944, he kept detailed journals about various happenings while in a prisoner of war camp, but also kept a detailed log of the letter "bashes" he received. He categorized them as "Friends," "Family," "Wanda," "Kin folks," and "Church Folks." He recorded the date each correspondence was written, when it was received, and the type of correspondence, either a letter or a greeting card.

According to Becky, this detailed correspondence did much to boost his morale letting him know that he was not alone in his struggles. The fact that these pieces of paper made it back to the USA is testament to their importance. Forced to march out of Stalag Luft III across Poland and Germany into a biting storm that had already dropped six inches of snow on the ground, the POW's were ill equipped for exposure to Europe's coldest winter on record in 50 years. With little room to carry belongings, Morris wore layers of clothing, carried a meager supply of food, two cartons of cigarettes, his Bible given to him by the International YMCA, his journals, a paper program showing his participation in South Compound's production of Handel's Messiah in December 1944, and those precious letters and cards from home.

Dear Sammie
How's my buddy?
Well Sammie I am
Really Busy these
days. I don't have
much time to write
any more.
Hope you like
This CARD.
Your Buddy
MORRIS

Mr. Sammie Bratton
129 E. Emerald Ave.
Knoxville,
Tennessee

U. S. Army Pursuit Plane [Multiplace] in Fl

How's Sammie
Here is a picture of one of
the Army's best Pursuit Planes.
Well I had a Slight cold since
I've been here hope you are Staying
Well these days. Tell your Grand
Mother and MRS Bratton Hello.
Your Buddy. MORRIS

MR. Sammie BRATTON
129 E. Emerald Ave
Knoxville, Tenn.

TRAINING PLANES FOR BOMBARDIERS & NAVIGATORS

(cont. from page 214) reports of the attack on Pearl Harbor. Like many others, Morris quickly enlisted. He was also good friends with the young Sam E. Bratton, Jr. the son of Sam E. Bratton, Sr., the pastor of Emerald Avenue Methodist Church. Epps sent these postcards home to little Sammie while he was stationed in Laredo and San Antonio, Texas for bomber training school. Sam E. Bratton Sr. married Wanda and Morris at the church in 1943 during a 10-day delay in route after Morris was commissioned a 2nd Lt. in Texas and before he reported to Salt Lake Army Air Base. *Postcards courtesy Sam E. Bratton, Jr. Story from Becky Lawson, daughter of Morris Epps.*

He was limited in his ability to respond to such correspondence, only four postcards and three letters each month. Naturally, he reserved most of those for his young wife, Wanda. But the following letters from Pastor Samuel E. Bratton to Lieutenant Morris F. Epps during his imprisonment share a great deal about the Oakwood community, the community of faith at Emerald Avenue Methodist Church, and how people of this community can look out for one another, even across an ocean during a terrible time of war.

Letter to 2nd Lt. Morris F. Epps, Stalag Luft 3, Germany

typewritten letter from:
Mr. Samuel Edward Bratton, 129 E Emerald Avenue, Knoxville, Tennessee

(Ch. No. 2)("Approximately"?)"APP" circled with pencil, Sept. 7 or 3 pencilled in afte
(postmark not readable) (received Oct. 13, 1944)

Dear Morris:
Well, after the hot weather this cool spell
is really invigorating. Makes a fellow feel a
little younger anyway. I am still working on the
church debt and really believe we will have it off
by Conference time. It is almost down to $1400.00
now and there is around eight hundred in sight.
We sold the old pews to the Methodist church in
Bland, Va. but they have not sent for them yet.
We got $150.00 for them. We have all of the seats
we need to replace them and I think it was a good
idea to get rid of them. The Board of Stewards
met last Tuesday and set the salary for the pastor
at $2520.00 for the ensuing year. Fred is doing
some painting in the Beginner's Department now.
It is really looking good. After we get our debt
all off we hope we can do more of that kind of
work. Conference will be held the eleventh of
October at Church St. We have arranged to have
six delegates. It may be that we will need to
take a few more. I was over to see your mother
this evening. They are all getting along fine.
All of our church finances will be up to date at
Conference time as usual. Our only hard pull will
be the churh debt. The committee is about ready
to start working on that in earnest now.
My small son is enjoying his bicycle these days.
I plan to put it in the car and take them to the
country soon so the traffic will not molest him
so much.
We have a Children's day program here next Sun.
All of the departments are taking part in it this
year. Then, on the first Sunday in Oct.we will
have the candle light Communion service which all
of the members enjoy so much.
I have just finished getting the bulletin, or
church program, out. As the membership grows it
continues to take more of my time, but it helps
for them to have a printed program. Love, Sam.

Prisoner of War. Lt. Morris Epps as he appeared on his POW identification card. *Photo courtesy Wanda Epps.*

Letter to 2nd Lt. Morris F. Epps, Stalag Luft 3, Germany

typewritten letter from:
Mr. Samuel Edward Bratton, 129 E Emerald Avenue, Knoxville, Tennessee

(Ch. No. 4)(postmark, Sept.16, 1944, 3PM, New York, N.Y.)(received Oct. 27,1944)

Dear Morris:
Well, it was refreshing to have your wife over
with us last Sunday. She looks just like she did
the day the marriage ceremony was performed.
I have a lot of things to do here in order to be
ready for our annual meeting of the church. Our
District Supt. will be with us Fri. Sep. 22 for
our last Quarterly Conference. I think a lot of
him. We were in school together at Emory, Va.
We had our Children's day program last Sun. a.m.
Mrs. Hacker and Christine did not attend. Did I
tell you that the stewards raised the salary $10
per month for next year? They also plan to pay
the full acceptance on Missions, which is $400.00.
We are really expecting to have the church debt
off by Oct. but Bishop Kern will not be able to
have the dedication before next summer. That will
give us time to do some re-decorating in the Sunday School departments. We are doing right well
to have such a small number of members. Since
Earl Watkins is with us we are having a double
quartet on Sunday mornings. Bob Rogers is a good
singer and I found a Mr.Farley on N. Fourth last
evening who sings. His father and I were in
school together. They have been here for several
months, but I didn't find them until recently.
Mrs.Farley is teaching in a High School just out
of town somewhere. Every one seems to be keeping
well around here. It had been a long time since I
have had a funeral. Guess some one has told you
that Mabel Lyons and Eugene Mason were married.
They bought a home in S. Knoxville and are living
there. Mr. & Mrs. West are moving into the 200 block
of Oakhill. They bought from Mrs. Acuff. I met Mrs.
West coming to clean house this a.m. at 6:00 when I
was out delivering church bulletins. Morris, we are
certainly glad that you are well. We shall continue
to remember you and I shall try to write my usual
weekly letter to you. Your mother and all are fine.
I see them every week. Best Wishes, S.E. BRATTON

Letter to 2nd Lt. Morris F. Epps, Stalag Luft 3, Germany

typewritten letter from:
Mr. Samuel Edward Bratton, 129 E Emerald Avenue, Knoxville, Tennessee

(Ch. No. 5) (postmark, Aug. 31, 1944, 5PM, Knoxville,Tenn)(received Nov. 8, 1944)

Aug. 31, 1944

Dear Morris:
It is needless for me to tell you that we were
delighted to get a call from your wife telling
us that she had gotten a card from you telling her
that you were well & also that the food was very
good. We just know that you will get along just
fine because of your spirit of brotherliness
toward all men everywhere.
Everything is about as usual here, Elizabeth
Mason and "Bob" Rogers are being married at
Emerald Ave. today. Earl Watkins is singing there
Sun. a.m. He is not singing any where else now.
I had a good long talk with him recently here &
he had quit drinking. He brought the three boys
to Sunday School Sun. & he and his wife were at
church. It really does me good to be able to
help any-one.
The church debt is down to sixteen hundred dollars.
I do not know how much more will be paid before
Conference, but it will be some smaller by then.
I see most of your folks every week. They are getting along nicely. Next Sun. I am taking dinner
with the Lion's, and last Sun. I was over at
Clacks on Marion St.
I have been helping Sam Ed get his bike rigged
up this week. We painted it blue & I sewed a new
seat cover on it. My painting did very well, but
my sewing wasn't so good, however I think it will
work. School starts today, so he will not get to
ride much except on Sat. and only then when I
take him where the traffic is light.
"Dick" Douglass has shingles, but seems to be
getting along very well. I forgot to tell you
that "Bob "Rogers put his church membership here.
He is attending school at the University. We are
glad that you can have religious services in your
camp. Our prayers go out daily for you.
Well, Morris, I must be getting ready for the
wedding. It seems only yesterday since we had
one here for you and Wanda. S.E. Bratton

Letter to 2nd Lt. Morris F. Epps, Stalag Luft 3, Germany

typewritten letter from:
Mr. Samuel Edward Bratton, 129 E Emerald Avenue, Knoxville, Tennessee

(Ch. No. 6) (postmark Sept. 26, 1944, PM, New York, N.Y.) (received Nov. 8, 1944)

Dear Morris:
This is certainly a busy time getting all of the
church reports ready for our annual meeting
at Church Street Church. Money is coming in from
everywhere, seemingly, on the church debt. It now
is down to less than eight hundred and we know
where most of that is coming from. Our Dictrict
Superintendent, Dr. Rudy, is paying one hundred.
We will make all payments easy these last two
Sundays. I am expecting most of it to come in
tomorrow. How do you suppose we will feel with a
debt free church after carrying the load for
more than twenty years? I have been living with
this debt so long, and talking (about) it so much that I
can imagine I will be rather lonely without it,
but I believe I can find something else to do.
This will give me more time to get in touch with
unsaved persons. Our Janitor is still keeping
the lawn and church looking good. He has finished
painting the two rooms used by the Beginners. They
look real good. We want to get more of that done
before the Bishop comes to dedicate the church.
I have had a bad cold for a few days, but shall
try to preach tomorrow anyway. If it doesn't get
better soon, I shall have a Doctor to do a paint
job on it. Our Young People went on a truck to
take a hay ride this week, but it started raining
before they got to the farm, so they had to come
back. The truck broke down on Western Ave. so a
bunch of us were out until after twelve o'clock
that night in cars trying to get them all in.
We shall continue to remember you in our prayers
and I know you have been remembering us, because
God has had a big part in the work that has been
done in our church this year. We are certainly
glad to know that you are getting along so well.
There are likely to be a few changes in ministers
at Conference, but so far as I know I will be
back on the job here. With all best wishes to you
from all at the church. Bro. Sam.

Letter to 2nd Lt. Morris F. Epps, Stalag Luft 3, Germany

typewritten letter from:
Mr. Samuel Edward Bratton, 129 E Emerald Avenue, Knoxville, Tennessee

(Ch. No. 7) (postmark Oct. 5, 1944, PM, Knoxville, Tenn.) (received Nov. 20, 1944)

Dear Morris:
I just believe that I let last week slip by
without getting a letter to you. PERHAPS I
CAN DO BETTER IN THE FUTURE.
LAST SUNDAY WAS REALLY A DAY OF REJOICING FOR
US. AT LAST THE CHURCH HAS PAID EVERY DOLLAR
THAT IT OWNED THE BD. OF CHURCH EXTENSIONS.
WE HAD A REAL GOOD CONGREGATION. IT WAS ALSO
COMMUNION SUNDAY.
I THINK THE TRUSTEES PLAN TO BUY A PARSONAGE
BEFORE COLD WEATHER IF THEY CAN FIND ONE THAT
WILL BE SUITABLE.
MY SON IS SUPPOSED TO BE BACK FROM SCHOOL NOW.
SINCE HIS MOTHER IS AT A CHURCH MEETING I MUST
GO UP THERE TO MEET HIM.
WITH LOVE FROM ALL. S.E. BRATTON.

Bombardier, Pilot and Co-Pilot. Lt. Morris Epps, bombardier, Lt. Beck Beckman, pilot, and co-pilot Lt. Chuck Yant pose in this stateside photograph before they deploy to Europe, where they are shot down over Germany. *Photo courtesy Wanda Epps.*

Home At Last. Morris and Wanda Epps visit Abingdon, Virginia with Emerald Avenue Methodist Pastor Sam Bratton Sr. and his wife Irene in April, 1945 after Morris is liberated from a German POW camp. *Photo courtesy Wanda Epps.*

Emerald Youth Foundation: a Legacy of the Epps Family

For the last ten years, the Emerald Grant has been awarded to a high school senior who has been a faithful participant in the ministry of the Emerald Youth Foundation. The grant program is administered as part of JustLead, a network of nine churches and faith-based organizations that offer JustLead, the flagship program of the Emerald Youth Foundation, to youth in neighborhoods across the city. The Emerald Grant is made possible by the Epps family. The recipients have been:

2000 — Elizabeth Rene Dunn

2001 — Amy L. Shields

2002 — Kyla Easterday

2003 — Rachel Shields

2004 — Sarah Scarbrough

2005 — Marissa Murray-Dalton

2006 — Andrew Harrison and Brandi Ashburn

2007 — Robert Thompson

2008 — Crystal Brown

2009 — Miranda Odom

2010 — Keisha Gordan

Loe Keisling Scarborough. Portrait of Keisling Scarborough, age 17, taken in 1911. Loe married Mark (Marcus) A. Scarborough, Sr. December 20, 1911. She lived over 90 years at 221 East Quincy Avenue, passing away in 1992. *Photo courtesy Edna Mae Frances Scarborough.*

Portraits

This last chapter really defies any other definition other than as purely neighborhood art. In an antique shop, my wife and I often joke about the fact that if you don't have a large number of historic photos of your family, you could always buy some framed photos in an antique shop and just invent new family members.

"Yep, that's Aunt Sally. There's Uncle Edward. Just bought 'em last week."

Seriously though, these rare portraits, many of them very early 20th century images, are total nostalgia, and a book about Oakwood-Lincoln Park would not be complete without them. While the community doesn't have a long list of famous residents now passed on, these treasured photographs leave a clue about the status and importance of some of these families and their ability to commission such fine portraits.

Which is your favorite one?

W.H. Baldock and Willie Baldock. This 1912 portrait of W.H. Baldock and Willie Baldock. Willie was the first president of the PTA at Christenberry Junior High School in 1936. She also started the Oakwood Garden Club. W.H. Baldock was active at Emerald Avenue Methodist Church. He was a sheet metal worker for the railroad traveling frequently for the sheet metal workers union. They lived at 602 East Oak Hill Avenue before St. Mary's Hospital was built. *Photo courtesy Biddy Leahy.*

Mark and Loe Scarborough. Wedding portrait of Mark Scarborough Sr. and Loe Keisling Scarborough, December 20, 1911. *Photo courtesy Edna Mae Frances Scarborough.*

Reece, Etolee, and Clarence Cox. Reece, Etolee and Clarence Cox, children of Bill and Sally Cox Reece, Etolee, and baby Clarence Cox in the yard of the family home in the 300 block of Caldwell circa 1908. *Photo courtesy Marsha Robbins.*

William and Sally Cox. Parents of Reece, Etolee and Clarence Cox. *Photo courtesy Larry Cox.*

Mrs Sylvan Love. Mrs Sylvan Love and her daughter Betty, born in 1932. The Loves lived in the first block of Morelia Avenue west of Harvey Street. Behind them stood the CB Atkin Mantel Co. and Van Gilder Mirror (later silver manufacturing). *Photo courtesy Harold Elkins.*

Liza Loftis. Liza Loftis sits on her porch on Harvey Street circa 1915. *Photo courtesy Jennifer Montgomery.*

Baby John Gilmer. An early baby portrait of John R. Gilmer, father of Sam Gilmer, possibly 1890s. *Photo courtesy Ann Watson.*

The Scarboroughs. The extended Scarborough family. Front row: Marley S. Duncan, 1871-1931; William Venson Scarborough, 1836-1899; Sarah Cross Scarborough, 1841-1908;   Calvin Scarborough, 1867-1940. Back row: Delia S. Sherrod, 1881-1937; Lillie S. McCampbell, 1876-1956; Charley Scarborough, 1879-1959; Johnny Scarborough, 1869-1948; Mark Scarborough, 1874-1966; Ada S. Letsinger, 1872-1913. *Photo courtesy Edna Mae Frances Scarborough.*

Brothers in Arms. Carroll and Louis Hassell. Carroll became the North Knoxville postman for many years and passed away in 2003. Louis died very young in a Boy Scout accident at Lyons Bend in West Knoxville. *Photo courtesy Jennifer Montgomery.*

Loe Keisling. Portrait of 9 year old Loe Keisling and her mother September, 1904. Loe's parents lived in the Wolf Valley section of Anderson County. *Photo courtesy Edna Mae Frances Scarborough.*

Sugar and Spice and Everything Nice. 1901 portrait of Loe Keisling age 6 and Cora Harrell, age 9. The dog's name was Sport. Note the china dolls the girls are holding. *Photo courtesy Edna Mae Frances Scarborough.*

Oakwood Mayor Rufus Underwood. Family gathering at Edgar and Ethel Underwood's house at 332 Oak Hill Avenue. Uncle Rufus and Aunt Emma Underwood are in this portrait. Rufus was mayor of Oakwood. *Photo courtesy Edna Mae Frances Scarborough.*

Hassell Men. Carroll Hassell and his father William Hassell in front of the family home on either Springdale or Burwell. William was a stone cutter on North Central and Carroll worked for the postal service. *Photo courtesy Jennifer Montgomery.*

Carroll Hassell. Postal Service portrait of Carroll Hassell possibly 1940's. While there are quite a few images of Carroll Hassell in this book, from a baby to a grown man, the Hassell images offered important views of several streetscapes of the area, including the cover image of the book. *Photo courtesy Jennifer Montgomery.*

Appendix A: A Trip to Churchwell's Farm

by Harvey Lee Ross, 1899

And now perhaps some of the readers want to know how it happened that I, a resident of Illinois, ever came to know and learn very much about Andrew Jackson, who lived in Tennessee, and what led me to make him a visit at the Hermitage. So I will have to go into some family affairs to show how it happened. So I would say in the first place that all of my wife's relation back of the present generation were Tennesseeans and were raised but a short distance from where Gen. Jackson lived, and they all knew him. My wife's father, Charles Kirkpatrick, who lived near Canton, Ill., and was an elder in the Presbyterian church of that place for many years, was a captain under Gen. Jackson in the war of 1812, and was with him in many expeditions against the Creek and Chickasaw Indians, and knew the old hero from his youth up. My wife's uncle (a brother to her mother), Col. George W. Churchwell, a prominent lawyer in that part of the country where General Jackson lived, had held the appointment of Indian agent under Jackson during a part of his presidential administration, and had practiced law at the bar with him, and had practiced law before the general when he was judge. Col. Churchwell's wife was also well acquainted with Jackson, and knew him at the time when he was converted and united with the Presbyterian church, and had sat at the communion table with him, herself being a Presbyterian. Now it was from these persons I got a good deal of my information about Gen. Jackson. Gen. Churchwell was widely known throughout that part of the country. In addition to his large law practice he was a farmer and breeder of fine stock. He had a farm of 500 acres two miles north of Knoxville, Tenn. At the time I visited him in 1843 he was the owner of some forty slaves of both sexes and all ages. Col. C. and wife came to Fulton county about every two years to visit his sister and family and to look after some lands he had there. It was on the occasion of one of those visits that I met with him and bargained for some of his fine stock. So in the fall of 1843 I started from Havana, Ill., with two horses and a carriage, in company with my wife's brother, Alexander Kirkpatrick, and my brother, Pike C. Ross, to go to Knoxville to bring home the stock. But before we started Captain Kirkpatrick charged us very particularly if we traveled near to the Hermitage to be sure to stop and see Gen. Jackson and to give to the old general his kind regards, and to tell him the number of his regiment and company, and what battles and expeditions they were in together.

I stated in my last communication that with my brother Pike C. Ross and my wife's brother, A. C. Kirkpatrick, I had made arrangements to go to Knoxville, Tennessee, to bring home some fine stock that I had purchased of my wife's uncle, Col. George W. Churchwell, who lived on a farm near that place. My brother Pike at that time was about eighteen years, and my wife's brother was two years older. Both were full of life and were desirous of getting as much pleasure out of the trip as possible.

We started from Havana, Mason county, about the first of October, 1843, with a span of fine traveling horses and a light carriage. Our route ran through a section of country where I had traveled as early as in 1829 and 30, and I could point out to the boys some of the old landmarks of that early day and tell them of the wonderful changes that had taken place in the country since I first traveled through it.

In 1828 when my father settled at Havana there was not a house on the Springfield road between Havana and Miller's Ferry on the Sangamon river, a distance of fifteen miles. And in all that section of country lying between the Sangamon river and the Mackinaw river and running east from the Illinois river for a distance of fifteen miles, containing at least 400 square miles, there was not a white inhabitant except three or four families at Havana. Great numbers of Indians lived along the water course, and their Indian ponies by the thousands ranged over all that vast country.

As we traveled on we stopped at the old town of New Salem, Mr. Lincoln's old home and stamping ground, where he kept store and the post office. I had not been there since I carried the mail some ten years before, and I wanted to see how the old town looked. I found some of the old buildings still standing, but most of them had been taken to Petersburg. Mr. Lincoln's house, where he kept store and the post office, and Samuel Hill's store, where Mr. Lincoln had clerked, had been taken away. The old log tavern where Mr. Lincoln and I boarded was still there, and I wanted to patronize it for Auld Lang Syne's sake, but the old sign with "The New Salem Inn" on it had been taken down and we could get no accommodations. The frame of the water mill was still standing, but there was no longer a mill there. There is a little history about that mill and the men who built it which I will relate: It was at this mill that Mr. Lincoln first got employment when he came to New Salem, and it was at this mill that Samuel Hill had 100 barrels of flour made which Mr. Lincoln took to New Orleans on his flat boat. The mill was built by John Cameron and George Rutledge, who were also the proprietors of New Salem. John Cameron sold his interest in the mill and moved to Fulton county and settled on the bluffs half a mile south of where Bernadotte now stands. He was one of the proprietors of Bernadotte. He built a water mill at that place which was the first grist mill ever built on Spoon river. He moved from Fulton County to Oregon, and from there to California. He died in Oakland, California. His grandson W. W.

Cameron, represented Oakland in the state legislature, and was also mayor of Oakland.

The next place we came to that is worth mentioning was old Sangamontown, lying on the Sangamon river, and about eight miles from Springfield. It was laid out about the same time that Springfield was. It was at this place that Mr. Lincoln built the flat boat which he took to New Orleans, and it was at this place that Peter Cartwright organized his first church and Sabbath school after coming to Illinois. His residence was on a farm two miles south of town.

We went on to Springfield and there took the old stage road that ran from Springfield to Vandalia. I remember traveling that road in 1829 in company with my father and a hired man. We were taking a drove of horses from Havana to St. Louis for sale, as that place was at that time the principal market for all Illinois. There was not a house or habitation from Springfield to Macoupin, a distance of eighteen miles. The whole country was covered with high grass, in many places extending above the backs of our horses. And then there was another thing that happened to us that I will never forget. It was the terrible fight we had with the horseflies. It appeared as if that whole country was swarming with horseflies. There was the small fly that would cover the head and ears of the horses, the green-headed and large black fly. They would torment the poor horses so that they would run into the high grass and roll over to get rid of them. Sometimes a half dozen would be down at once. We had hard work to keep the horses we rode from doing the same thing. When we got to Macoupin Point we were told that our trip across the prairie ought to have been made in the night, that during the summer season the stages and most all travelers crossed the prairie at night to avoid the flies.

When we left Sangamon we struck through for Vandalia, where the capital of the state had been located for many years before it was removed to Springfield. I had a strong desire to visit the old town of Vandalia that I had heard so much talk about. For a number of years after the settlement of the country all the land in the state owned by individuals upon which the taxes had not been paid were sold for the taxes at Vandalia. I remember that my father and Joel Wright of Canton and a few other men of Fulton county were in the habit of going to Vandalia to attend these sales. My brother Lewis lived at Vandalia at one time about a year. It was in 1828 or '29. He went there to learn the printer's trade. He held the position I think of what that craft calls the "printer's devil." He worked for Judge James Hall, who was one of the first editors in the state. I think he moved out of the state and my brother gave up the trade. It was at Vandalia where Mr. Lincoln first went to the legislature, and Major Newton Walker was a member at that same time from Fulton county. From Vandalia we traveled southeast to the Ohio river. We found the country from Vandalia to the river settled generally by people who emigrated from the salve-holding-states, and the improvements were much inferior to the country we had passed between Springfield and Vandalia. Where the country had been settled mostly by eastern people in the southern part of the state a great many people were still living in their log houses, and small farms in cultivation; part of their land was planted in tobacco, cotton and flax. The southern counties had been settled much longer than the northern and middle counties, but were far behind in improvements. I will mention a little circumstance that happened as we were traveling through that part of the country, which was a little amusing to my young companions, and will demonstrate the amount of enterprise the people possessed:

We stopped one day at a farm house to get a drink of water, and the lady of the house came out with a gourd that would hold a half gallon and told us that if we wanted a good cool drink that we had better go to the well, and pointed to where it was, and remarked that if we found any polliwigs in the water we were to pound the gourd against the side of the ladder that was in the well and they would all go to the bottom. So my brother Pike climbed down the well on the ladder and found the water alive with polliwigs, but he obeyed instructions and pounded the gourd against the side of the ladder and the polliwigs all disappeared and he brought up the gourd full of water without a polliwig or tadpole in it.

We went on the Ohio river and was informed that the best way to go Knoxville in Tennessee was to go through Nashville. So when we got to Nashville we put up at the City Hotel, which we found afterwards was the very hotel where the wonderful tragedy had taken place between General Jackson and the Bentons, where Jackson, in attempting to horsewhip Thomas H. Benton, was shot by Jesse Benton, a brother of Thomas, putting a ball through his arm and one in his shoulder. The particulars of the fight and the cause of it I will give further on.

On our arrival at Nashville, as stated last week, we put up at the City Hotel, where the terrible tragedy had taken place between General Jackson and the two Bentons. The landlord had kept the hotel for a good many years, and was well acquainted with Gen. Jackson. There were also several men staying at the hotel who had been personally acquainted with Gen. Jackson for twenty or thirty years, and they gave us a good deal of information about him and the circumstances of the fight, as follows:

Thomas H. Benton, the old United States senator, who, I believe, served longer in the senate than any other man, had a brother Jesse who lived in Nashville, and who had got into some trouble with another Nashville man named Wm. Carroll. Jesse Benton sent Carroll a challenge to fight, and he accepted the challenge. Carroll and Jackson were warm friends, he having served under Jackson in the army as captain. So he went out to the Hermitage to see if Jackson would act as his second in the duel, but Jackson objected, saying that he was a friend of the Bentons and he did not want to do anything that would offend them. But he told Carroll that he would go to Nashville, and see Jesse Benton and try to have the matter settled between them without any fighting, and he came to town and tried to have the matter settled between them. But Benton gave him to understand that Capt. Carroll would have to fight or show the white feather, saying that he would run him out of town. Benton made use of some language that Jackson thought was rather insulting, and so he consented to act as Carroll's second in the duel. They went out and took a crack at each other. Benton was wounded quite severely in the side, though not dangerously, and Capt. Carroll was slightly wounded in the left thumb. Benton was laid up twenty days with his wound. Thomas H. Benton the brother of Jesse was in Washington city at the time of the duel. When he received the news that his brother Jesse had fought a duel with Capt. Carroll and was badly wounded, and that Carroll had but a slight wound in his left thumb, and that General Jackson had been a second to his brother's antagonist, his wrath and indignation knew no bonds, and not having the facts in the case, he wrote Jackson very insulting and abusive letters, accusing him of all kinds of treachery and dishonesty, and some of his letters were published in the Nashville papers. These things aroused all the old tiger there was in Gen. Jackson and while his wrath and high temper had the control of his better judgment he made a solemn vow in the presence of some friends that, "By the eternal, the first time I get my eyes on Tom Benton I will horsewhip him!" So in about a month after the duel was fought Thomas H. Benton came to Nashville and put up at the City Hotel. His brother Jesse by that time had recovered from his wound so that he was able to walk about the streets. In a few days after, Gen. Jackson rode to town to get his mail, left his horse at the Nashville Inn, but kept his horsewhip in his hand. After he got his mail he walked past the City Hotel and there observed Thomas H. Benton and his brother Jesse standing in the front of the hotel a-talking. He walked up to Benton and told him that he had to take back those scandalous assertions that he had made about him or he would have to take a horsewhipping. At that Benton made some pretense as if he were going to draw a pistol. Jesse Benton, who was standing near, seeing the predicament that his brother was in and with little chance to defend himself, drew his pistol and blazed away at Jackson and brought him to the ground, pistol, horsewhip and all. His pistol was loaded with two balls, one of which went through Jackson's arm and the other lodged in his shoulder. Jackson carried that ball in his shoulder for twenty years. The fight created a wonderful excitement in Nashville. The news ran like wildfire, and in ten minutes after Jackson was shot a thousand men were at the hotel and many fights took place between the friends of the two parties. One of Jackson's friends knocked Jesse Benton down and pounded him almost to death. Thos. H. Benton in the fight and skirmishing fell through an open doorway into the basement of the hotel, which saved him from getting a terrible whipping. The landlord told us that Jackson was confined at the hotel about three weeks before he could be removed to his home.

Soon after this occurrence Thos. H. Benton left the state of Tennessee and moved to Missouri, and he and Jackson did not meet again until sixteen years after, when they met as senators in Washington and had selected seats, unknown to either of them, that were located side by side; and they were both placed on some important committee, so that they had to come face to face. But they at once shook hands and were forever after good friends.

The next morning we started on our way to the Hermitage, which was some ten or eleven miles from Nashville. We traveled on a fine turnpike road which ran through a fertile country. On the road between Nashville and the Hermitage we passed the spot where there had been built at one time a fort or blockhouse, where the people gathered when the Indians were troublesome. The fort, we were told, was afterwards purchased by Gen. Jackson and a man named Coffee and converted into a storehouse, and there they kept store for some years under the name of Jackson & Coffee. They bought large quantities of cotton and produce and shipped it down the Cumberland and Mississippi rivers in flatboats to New Orleans. Near the fort was one of the finest racetracks in the state, and there they also had a place erected for the exhibition of game cocks, where people came from hundreds of miles and from other states with their race horses and game cocks. Thousands of dollars would be bet on the races and cock fights.

We found the Hermitage was located about a half a mile from the turnpike road that ran from Nashville to Knoxville, but he had a private road that ran from the turnpike up to his house. Before we got to his house we passed a small brick Presbyterian church which we were told that Gen. Jackson had built on his own land for the accommodation of his wife after she united with that church; and it was at this little church where he was converted and joined the Presbyterian church, of which I may have something more to say. We drove up to the house and hitched our horses, opened the little iron gate and went in. We found the general sitting on his front piazza reading a newspaper. We introduced ourselves to him as well as we could, and told him we were from Illinois and on our way to Knoxville to take home some fine stock that I had purchased from Col. George W. Churchwell of that place, and told him of our relationship to Capt. Charles Kirkpatrick, who had served under him, and gave him the number of the regiment and the company that he commanded. The general said he remembered him very well, and told us of several expeditions they had been on together, and appeared to be pleased that we had called to see him, and asked us to have our horses put up and stay to dinner with him. But I told him as it was early in the day we would rather drive a few miles further before dinner. He said he was always glad to hear from any of the old comrades who were with him in the army, and was glad to meet any of their relatives. He asked my brother-in-law a good many questions about his father; want to know in what part of Illinois he lived, what his occupation was, and how many children he had. He said he knew his father very well, and also his two brothers then living in Tennessee. He also said he was very well acquainted with his uncle, George W. Churchwell, who had held the office of Indian agent when he was president, and had practiced law before him when he was judge. He also said that he knew his aunt, Col. Churchwell's wife; that they were both Presbyterians. He asked us if we would take a walk with him out in his orchard, saying he had some pretty good eating apples. But before we went to the orchard he took us through several rooms of his house. In one room he had a large library of books, with a number of fine pictures hanging around the walls. In another room he had a great lot of old war relics, such as old swords, pistols and old muskets, all the flint locks, and a great lot of old regimental clothing that was hanging around the walls. Some of it looked like it might have been worn in the times of the Revolutionary War. The Hermitage was a good, substantial building, but everything about it was very plain. Such a house could have been built in Illinois at that time for $4,000. He told me that his wife's nephew, Mr. Donelson and family, were living with him. He took us to his barn and showed us a span of carriage horses that he had, but they were not as good as the span I was driving. His barn was quite plain—no better than many Illinois farmers had at that time. We went from the barn to the orchard. He had a very fine orchard and a most excellent quality of fruit. He told us to tie up in our handkerchiefs and take all the apples we wanted to eat on our way. So we laid in a pretty fair supply which lasted till we got across the mountains. I told the general that he had some good eating apples and that I would like to take a half dozen home to my wife and boy; that I had a boy sixteen months old, and I could tell them when I got home that the apples came from Gen. Jackson's orchard. So he took me to a tree of large red apples which he called winesaps; so I gathered the apples and stored them away carefully in my satchel and brought them home. As we were returning from the orchard to the house he took us through a lot that lay a few rods east of the house and there showed us the grave of his wife. It was a plat of ground about 8x10 feet, enclosed with a marble wall rising about three feet above the ground, and a partition wall in the middle; on one side his wife was laid and was covered with a marble slab on which was engraved, "Mrs. Rachel Jackson, died 23rd December, 1828, aged sixty-one years." The general told us that when he died that he expected to be laid by his wife in the enclosed plat of ground. He spoke of his poor health and said that he did not think it would be many months until he would be lying there. He was very thin in flesh and pale at that time. He had us come into the house again and brought in a pitcher of cold water. I asked him if he had ever been in Illinois. He said he had not, but he had become acquainted with a good many Illinois men when he was in Congress and while he was president, and named over several that I knew. He also said that he had been acquainted with a Methodist preacher who had been a delegate to the Nashville conference by the name of Peter Cartwright, who was now living in Illinois, and asked me if I knew him. I told him that I knew him very well; that he had often staid at my father's house and had preached in our log cabin in the early pioneer times, before there were any church buildings put up. He then went on and told the story that when Cartwright was preaching one time in Nashville he went to hear him, and as he was walking down the aisle the preacher in the pulpit by the side of Cartwright gave his coat a jerk and told him that Gen. Jackson was coming in; at which Cartwright spoke out so loud that all the church could hear him: "Who is Gen. Jackson? If he don't get his soul converted God will damn him as quick as He would a Guinea negro!" I suppose the general thought I had never heard the story; but I heard it some years before from the Cartwright side, and was pleased to hear it from the other side.

The general went down to the carriage with us to see our horses, and admired them very much, for they were splendid animals. He told us to give his kind regards to Col. Churchwell and wife when we got to Knoxville, and also to Capt. Charles Kirkpatrick when we got home.

There was one circumstance which I omitted to mention relating to my visit to the Hermitage, which was the splendid arrangement which Jackson had made for the pleasure and good of his slaves. Each family had a one-story frame house that was painted either white or red, and with it about an acre of ground, all fenced in with palings or board fence and whitewashed; and around each of these houses were a lot of fruit trees and shrubbery. We were told that the general was always good and kind to his slaves, and would never permit any of them to be sold to go to the southern states, and that his slaves were strongly attached to him, and that nothing would induce them to leave their old master. Notwithstanding the terrible temper that the general possessed, which made him like a Kansas cyclone when he was imposed upon and aroused, he still possessed a kind and tender heart. Many people told us, who had known the general and his good wife during all their thirty-seven years of married life, that she was a grand and noble Christian lady, and was honored and loved by everybody; that their affection for each other was of the tenderest kind; that the general always treated her as if she was his pride and glory, and that words could faintly describe her devotion to him; that it was seldom that a husband and wife lived as happily together as they had done. We were told that when Mrs. Jackson died no such demonstration had ever been known at a funeral in that part of the country before; that the mayor of Nashville issued a proclamation requesting business men to close their stores and asked that the bells of the city be tolled from 1 to 2 P. M., during the funeral. Every vehicle in the city was employed in taking people to the Hermitage, where the funeral was held. It was estimated that 10,000 people attended the funeral. The death of Mrs. Jackson was a terrible shock to the general, and some of his slaves went almost frantic with grief and despair. Such weeping and wailing had never been heard at a funeral, nor so much affection shown by slaves on the death of a mistress.

There was a little circumstance that took place in connection with the life of Gen. Jackson that I thought I would mention. I heard my father-in-law, Capt. Charles Kirkpatrick, speak of it, and also his brothers and some others that we met on our visit to Tennessee. It was on one of Gen. Jackson's expeditions against the Cherokee Indians, and will show that he did possess a kind and tender heart. The general and his soldiers were pursuing a band of Indians, and surrounded them; and as the Indians were attempting to escape every one was killed. In going to their wigwams they discovered a little boy papoose, and as the soldiers were about to dispatch him, the general commanded them not to hurt the little boy. And he took the little Indian boy home with him, and raised him, and sent him to school, and became very much attached to him. The little Indian boy became very expert in the riding of racehorses. He could get more speed out of them than any rider in the country; as the general was keeping some racehorses at the time, the boy made himself quite useful to the general. When the boy got to be fifteen years old the general thought he had better learn a trade; so he took him around among the artisans and mechanics in Nashville to choose the trade that he would prefer; so he chose the trade of saddlery and harness-maker, but after working at it a year he died. It was thought that if he had lived that the general would have made provisions for him in his will.

In giving this story about Gen. Jackson and the little Indian boy I might with some propriety make use of a habit peculiar to Mr. Lincoln; after listening to a story told by a friend, he would say: "Now, that puts me in mind of a little anecdote," and would go on and relate one of his quaint and humorous stories to match the one told him. So the circumstance about Gen. Jackson and the Indian boy had brought to mind a similar circumstance that took place with Alexander Kirkpatrick, who was with me at the time we visited Gen. Jackson. Whether the story above told about Jackson and the Indian boy had any bearing o the story that I am about to tell I cannot say.

Alexander Kirkpatrick, in 1847, went to study medicine with Dr. W. H. Nance, at Vermont, Illinois, and in 1850 went to California, and practiced medicine in San Francisco and also in Redwood City. He became very eminent in his profession, having at one time the largest practice in San Francisco. In 1861 there was ordered out in California a regiment of soldiers to go into the northern border of the state to fight the Indians, who had been murdering a good many families. Dr. Kirkpatrick got the appointment of surgeon to go with the army. On that expedition they came upon the camp of the hostile Indians and surrounded them, and as they attempted to escape everyone was killed. The soldiers went inside of the wigwams and there found a little girl papoose. One of the soldiers was about to run his bayonet through her when Dr. Kirkpatrick jumped in before him and caught the little girl up in his arms and saved her life. Some of the soldiers who had lost relatives by the Indians were determined that she should share their fate; but the doctor drew his revolver and said that he would protect the girl at the risk of his life. He brought the little Indian papoose home and raised and educated her the same as he did his own children. The doctor told me that the child had so many droll and quaint ways about her and was so different from other children that he gave her the name of "Topsy," after the girl spoken of by Harriet Beecher Stowe in "Uncle Tom's Cabin." So she always went by the name of Topsy Kirkpatrick up to the time of her marriage with a white man. I have asked the doctor if he thought that the stories we heard in Tennessee about Jackson and the Indian boy had anything to do with his rescue of the Indian girl, and he said he thought that it had.

Dr. Kirkpatrick died in San Francisco in 1894, leaving a widow and two sons and three daughters and Topsy to mourn his loss. He was a kind-hearted, noble and generous man, and honored by all who knew him. He left a beautiful home to his family and life insurance to the amount of $20,000.

In continuing my narrative of the trip I took through Tennessee at the time I visited Gen. Jackson I may allude to incidents that will not greatly interest the general reader. But it will be remembered that I am writing these sketches chiefly for the benefit of my children, grandchildren and great-grandchildren, so the reader will pardon these departures from the main theme of these sketches.

So I will take up our line of travel from the time we bade Gen. Jackson goodby at the Hermitage and turned our horses' heads towards Knoxville. The first place we stopped at was Lebanon. I have read somewhere in divine history something about the cedars of Lebanon, and when we drove into town we began to think we had found that place. Lebanon contained about 1,000 inhabitants, and was built in the middle of a large cedar grove. Part of the houses were built of logs and part were frame. The logs were all cedar and the frame houses were all built of cedar; the roofs were covered with cedar shingles and the fences and gates were all of cedar. So we concluded that Lebanon was a very appropriate name for the town.

We stopped over night at a hotel on the top of the Cumberland mountains. I went out to the barn after supper to see how our horses had been cared for. This was my custom, as we had a long journey to make and a good deal depended upon the condition of our team. I asked the negro hostler how much corn he had fed the horses. He said he had given them six ears apiece. I told him that the should have fed them twice that amount, but he answered, "Massa, they are great big ears." I asked how large the ears were. He said that they were almost as long as his arm and as big around as his leg. Then I said I wanted to see some of that corn; so he took me to the crib and I saw that the negro was not far out of the way, for they were the most wonderful ears of corn in size that I had ever seen. There was about as much feed in one ear as in two ears of common corn. I asked the landlord how it was that such large corn would grown on top of the Cumberland mountains. He said that there was a dark sandy loam on the mountains—just the kind of soil to produce large corn. So I went to the crib and selected one of the largest ears I could find, and shelled it, and packed it away in my satchel, intending to bring it home and try it on our Illinois soil, as I was at that time carrying on a large farm a half mile east of Havana in Mason county. I planted the corn by itself so that it would not get mixed with the other corn, and from that planting I raised several bushels. The next year I planted part of it and distributed the balance among some of my neighbor farmers, as I wanted to have it introduced all over the county. They gave it the name of the "Tennessee Mammoth Corn." I am sure that after I commenced raising that corn that the yield to the acre was at least a third more than it had been with common corn. Afterwards many Fulton county farmers came over to Mason county to get their seed corn.

We finally arrived at Col. Churchwell's with everything in good trim. Our horses had stood the trip excellently. Col. Churchwell and wife and about half a dozen negro servants were ready to meet us as they had heard that we were coming. We still had on hand some of the apples that Gen. Jackson had given us and we distributed them among the colonel's family and the servants, as they all wanted to taste the apples because they had come from Gen. Jackson's orchard. We delivered the messages the general had sent to Col. Churchwell and wife, and that led them both to tell us some marvelous stories about the general, for they had known him most all their lives. The colonel told us of a time that he was attending court in a neighboring town and Gen. Jackson was the presiding judge. A certain man had committed a crime, and a warrant had been placed in the hands of the sheriff, and he had summoned a half dozen men to assist him in making the arrest, for the man was a desperate character and was armed with several pistols and a bowie knife. The sheriff came into court and reported to the judge that the man could not be taken—that he and his men could not afford to risk their lives with such a character. The judge then said to him, "Summons Andrew Jackson to assist in taking that man." The sheriff did so, and Jackson took his hat and walked out of the court house and across the street to where the man was surrounded by many friends. Judge Jackson walked up to him, put his hand on his shoulder, and said to him, "You are my prisoner; you must go with me to the court house." The man made no resistance but walked deliberately to the court house where the judge took the pistols and knife from him and handed them to the sheriff. The man was asked afterwards why he did not resist Gen. Jackson as he had done the other men. He said he could see fight in the eyes of the judge, but could not see it in the eyes of the other men.

It took place at the little brick church near the Hermitage that he had built for his wife soon after they were married. I was told that Jackson and his wife were regular attendants at church while she was living, and that he was always a friend to all religious institutions, and that all his ancestors, including his mother, were Presbyterians. I will quote a few sentences from the biography of Peter Cartwright to show what the old pioneer Methodist preacher had to say about him, as follows:

"Gen. Jackson was certainly a very extraordinary man. He was no doubt in his prime of life a very wicked man, but he always showed a great respect for the Christian religion and the feelings of religious people, especially ministers of the gospel. I will here relate a little incident that shows his respect for religion. I had preached one Sabbath near the Hermitage, and in company with several gentlemen and ladies went by special invitation to dine with the general. Among the company there was a young sprig of a lawyer from Nashville, of very ordinary intellect, and was trying very hard to make an infidel of himself. As I was the only preacher present the young lawyer kept pushing his conversation on me in order to get into an argument. I tried to evade an argument, in the first place considering it a breach of good manners to interrupt the social conversation of the company, and in the second place, I plainly saw that his head was much softer than his heart, and that there were no laurels to be won by vanquishing or demolishing such a combatant; I persisted in evading an argument. This seemed to inspire the young man with more confidence in himself, for my evasiveness he construed into fear. I saw Gen. Jackson's eyes strike fire as he sat by and heard the thrusts made at the Christian religion. At length the young lawyer asked me this question:

"'Mr. Cartwright, do you believe there is any such place as hell?'
"'Yes, sir; I do.'

"To which he responded:

"'Well, I thank God I have too much good sense to believe any such thing.'

"I was pondering in my mind whether I would answer him or not when Gen. Jackson for the first time broke into the conversation, and, directing his words to the young man, said with great earnestness:

"'Well, sir, I thank God that there is such a place of torment as hell.'

"This sudden answer, made with great earnestness, seemed to astonish the youngster, and he exclaimed:

"'Why, Gen. Jackson, what do you want of such a place of torment as hell?'

"To which the general replied, as quick as lightning:

"'To put such a rascal as you in that opposes and vilifies the Christian religion!'"

After a cordial welcome to myself and my two young comrades we had a delightful time going with Col. Churchwell over his splendid farm of 500 acres, located two miles north of Knoxville, Tennessee. His Negroes cultivated about 300 acres, and the balance was in timber and seeded down to blue grass. He was engaged in raising fine-blooded stock. He had a fine dwelling house and ten or twelve frame houses on his place that his slave families occupied. He had fine barns and stables, and all his buildings and improvements were very good. He had about forty slaves of both sexes and of all ages. He was good and humane to his slaves and would never permit any of them to be sold to go to the southern plantations. His nephew was his overseer, and he told me that he very seldom had to punish a slave. Col. Churchwell was a member of the Methodist church, and his wife was a Presbyterian. It was his habit to hold family prayers morning and evening and he asked a blessing at his table. He and his wife were regular attendants at church. Sometimes both would go to the Methodist church and then to the Presbyterian church. Many of the slaves were church members, some belonging to one church and some to the other. Both Col. Churchwell and his wife believed that slavery was a divine institution, and that there was no harm in owning slaves, and the only harm there was about it was the abuse sometimes shown them by their masters. There was a very radical difference of opinion among my wife's relatives in regard to slavery, for on her father's side I have never known any of them to buy or sell a slave, although many of them were able to do so; but on her mother's (Churchwell's) side I never knew any of them who would not buy slaves if they had the money to do so.

The colonel and his good wife, "Aunt Moody," as we called her, did everything in their power to make us have a good and happy time. Their southern hospitality was manifested in many ways.

As stated in my first letter, the colonel and his wife were in the habit of visiting relatives in Illinois every two or three years; and I think the last time they came was in 1856, when they visited my family at Vermont, Fulton county. Mrs. Churchwell was one of the kindest, best women I have ever known. She became very much attached to our oldest boy, Frank, who was then about half grown. She wanted

Frank to promise her that when he was grown that he would go to Tennessee and visit his old Aunt Moody. She promised him that she would have the negroes dance for him, as she did when his father and uncles visited her, and would make him have a grand and good time.

Well, as time rolled away the boy did go and visit his old aunt, but he did not go in just the way she expected him to come, and he took more company with him than his old aunt was in the habit of entertaining, and he did not wait until he was grown, as his aunt had told him to do.

When the civil war came on and an appeal was made for volunteers, the boy caught the war fever and had it very badly. Because he was so young we did all in our power to persuade him from becoming a soldier; but at last his parents gave their consent and he was enrolled as a member of the old 84th regiment Illinois volunteers, which was made up from men from Fulton and McDonough counties under Col. Waters of Macomb. The regiment was at once ordered to go to east Tennessee, and singular as it may seem took up their headquarters right on Col. Churchwell's fine farm. They certainly could not have found a better locality for a military post if they had searched the state over, for the place was well watered with springs and creeks, with plenty of timber, and with an abundance of houses, barns and stables, and everything that a regiment of men could desire for their comfort and convenience. Col. Waters took possession of their fine old mansion for headquarters of himself and staff, though he was generous enough to let Mrs. Churchwell retain a few of the rooms. Col. Churchwell had died about the commencement of the war, and his only son, William, was an officer in the confederate army, and was killed before the war closed. Mrs. C. with her nephew as overseer, and her negroes, were running her farm when the regiment came down upon them like a cloud of Kansas locusts would upon a fertile field, and with almost as great destruction. It was a terrible ordeal for the old lady to see her beautiful place desecrated, her fine house occupied by soldiers and the soldiers' tents spread over the field, and her fine carriage horses taken for cavalry horses, and her large Norman horses, which her negroes needed so badly to work the farm, taken to haul some old cannon around over the country; and when she would remonstrate against such treatment the officers would tell her that it was a military necessity. And when her corn and hay would be taken from her barns, and her rails burned, and her dairy and chicken house looted, and her cows milked by the "Yankee bluecoats," then she would lay her grievances before Col. Waters, and he would try to appease her wrath and indignation by telling her that it was a military necessity. These indignities caused her at last to express her mind quite freely as to what she thought of them; so they gave her the name of "old rebel," for she was very bitter against the whole union army.

One day the old lady asked Col. Waters where those fellows came from that had settled down upon her premises, and he told her they were from Illinois. She then told him she had relatives in Illinois by the names of Kirkpatrick and Ross, and wanted to know of the colonel if he had any soldiers by either name. The colonel told her there was a young lad in the regiment whose name was Frank Ross. She said she would like to see him; so the colonel sent one of his offices to hunt Frank up, and after a considerable search he was found in one of the camps frying chickens. He was told there was an old rebel woman up at headquarters who wanted to see him. Frank knew nothing about whose farm it was they were camping on; so he went to the house without any idea as to whom he would meet.

But when he came face to face with the "old rebel woman," lo and behold, it was his old Aunt Moody Churchwell—the good old aunt that had invited him to come and visit her, and had promised that when he came she would have the negroes dance and sing for him! But here he was, with a lot of companions, desecrating and wrecking her fine farm and frying her chickens!

But when she saw that he was really Frank, the kind and noble impulses of her heart came to her as in times past, and she showed him the utmost kindness, and told Col. Waters that if the boy should be wounded or get sick to send him to her house and that she would see that he was well taken care of.

Now I must go back and give a sketch of our visit at Col. Churchwell's, where we remained two weeks, visiting him and my wife's relatives in Tennessee. Before starting home the colonel wanted us to have a good time, so he gave us two grand diversions. The first was a negro corn-shucking and the other was a negro dance, or, as they called it, a "negro shindig." If any Northern man ever traveled in the South in slave days and missed a negro corn-shucking or a negro dance, he missed a good deal. The pile of corn was forty feet long, eight feet wide and four or five feet high. They divided it off into two piles and drove a stake in the middle, then chose sides and went at it with a rush.

The side that came out last in shucking its pile had to furnish the egg-nogg to treat the whole company. As soon as the negroes commenced shucking the corn, working like beavers, they also commenced singing their plantation songs, and they sang with so much force and power that they could be heard about a mile. While the negroes were thus engaged their wives were preparing for them a bountiful supper. I do not think I ever saw a happier set of people than they were. The colonel had on his negro quarters one house with a large room in it that he said his negroes used to hold meetings in on Sundays, when some white or black preacher would come out from Knoxville and preach for them, and they used the same room to hold their dances in. His rule was to let them have a dance the last Saturday night in each month. He said it encouraged them and made them better servants. So one evening before we came away he gathered the negroes together, men, women, boys and girls, to show us how they could dance. He had one old negro, Ned, who played the violin for them. He told us that he was seventy years old, and had played on "de fiddle" since he was a boy, and seemed to be very proud of his skill. The music and the dancing were both grand, and we looked on with a great deal of delight.

But the time had come for our departure homeward. I had sold the horses and carriage that we had taken with us, and we rode home some of the horses I bought of Col. Churchwell. We bought fourteen head—horses, mares, jacks and jennies. We traveled the first day thirty miles and stopped over night at Arthur Kirkpatrick's, a brother of my wife's father. He was keeping a country store and running a farm. He had some negroes hired to work on the farm, but told us that he would never buy or sell a slave. He had known Gen. Jackson for several years and told us many stories about him; in fact, we could hardly meet an old settler in that state but who could tell us more or less about him.

We came home a different route from the one we went out on. It was nearer, but not so good a road. We came back through Kentucky and through the grand prairies of eastern Illinois.

Sometimes we found it twenty miles between the houses. We struck the road we had gone out on at Springfield.

On our way home we passed Major Newton Walker and Hugh Lamaster, who had been to Kentucky and bought a herd of Durham cattle. I think they were the first blooded cattle ever brought into Fulton county. When we reached home I found my wife and little boy, Ossian, anxiously awaiting our arrival, for we had been gone six weeks, and it was a time of joy and rejoicing when we got home, for I had never been away from home before to exceed a day since he was born. And when I opened my satchel and took out the six large apples that Gen. Jackson had given me to take home to my wife and boy (as mentioned in my second letter), our little boy hardly knew whether they were to eat or play with, for he had never seen an apple before. At that time there was not a bearing orchard in Mason county. A few orchards had been planted out, but none of them had commenced to bear. But he soon found that they were good to eat, and his little teeth went for them with a vengeance. I told him that the apples came from Gen. Jackson's orchard—that Jackson had sent them to Ossian and his mother. He had just commenced to learn to talk, and he learned to pronounce the words "Jackson" and "apples" a little before any other words, and after the apples were gone he would often climb up in my lap and put his little arms around my neck and say, "Papa, go to Jackson and get more apples for Ossian." But the apples that came from the orchard of the old hero were the first and the last that he ever had the opportunity to put his little teeth into, for in six weeks after my return he was taken from us by that cruel disease, the croup. He was eighteen months old when he died. He was unusually smart and bright for one of his age, and his death was a terrible bereavement to us, for our very hearts and lives were wrapped up in our little boy. He was our first child, and no tongue could express the grief and sorrow that filled our hearts when he was taken away. Another incident about the child: On the first visit of Col. Churchwell and wife to us in 1842, the little fellow was about six months old. Mrs. Churchwell had a bright, new half-dollar bearing the date "1842." So she got a hole drilled through the rim of it, put a ribbon through it, and hung it around little Ossian's neck, saying it would be a keepsake from her and would show the year the boy was born and the year of their first visit to us. After the lad died his mother laid the coin away, intending to keep it as a sacred memorial as long as she lived, and did keep it for almost forty years. But it was stolen by a servant. His mother would have rather lost a $20 gold piece than that sacred coin.

After we got back from our trip I called on Father Kirkpatrick to give him a few tales of our trip and to tell him about his brother and sister, and the great number of nephews and nieces we had met out there, and how anxious they were for him and his wife to go out and make a visit, and of the kind invitation Gen. Jackson had sent, that if he came to Tennessee again to come and see him. This produced a desire in the old gentleman's heart that he would like to go back to his native state where he had spent his boyhood. So a year after he secured a fine, large horse and carriage and he and his wife made the trip from Canton, Ill., to Knoxville, Tenn., and back without any mishap or accident. He went by the Hermitage, but learned before he got there that the old General had died a few weeks before. But he stopped at the grave with reverence for the old hero with whom he had fought many battles against the Indians; and we may be sure that he paid to his friend and leader the tribute of his tears.

Epilogue

And now you know the story of the two little towns of Oakwood and Lincoln Park, and you've been able to glimpse life as it was in a good portion of the 20th century.

Walk the tree-lined streets and alleyways of this grand community. Breathe in the fresh cut grass at Christenberry ballfield while watching a new generation of children learn how to throw a ball.

Dream of opening a business on North Central, following in the grand tradition of the many successful business owners who have come before.

Don't forget the rich heritage and tradition of Oakwood-Lincoln Park. Share these stories with your neighbors. Learn them well and pass them on. They're your stories.

Acknowledgements

The author would like to thank the following people for their invaluable assistance in the preparation of this book: My son, Jacob McDaniel, for his enthusiasm in learning the art and science of book publishing; My wife, Faith Andes McDaniel, for her strength and patience; Paul and Norma Kelley, for sharing their vision; Harold Elkins and Becky French Brewer, for putting the pieces together; Betsy Chandler Drake, for her administrative acumen; Kelly Horner Priest, for her services as a photo editor; Steve Cotham, Danette Welch, and Sally Polhemus, for technical assistance from the McClung Historical Collection; Cathy Irwin, for her dazzling research; Dr. Charlie Faulkner, for his wise counsel; Dr. Joan Markel of the Frank H. McClung Museum of the University of Tennessee and her amazing maps; and Charlie Richmond and Virginia Douglas, for shedding new light on the early farms of North Knoxville (may you find even more minie balls and railroad buttons!)

I wish to thank the members of the Oakwood-Lincoln Park Neighborhood Association, Mara Harvey, president, for their enthusiasm and support for the project, as well as the 2010-2011 board members: Barbara Armstead, Vice President; Donna Watson, Secretary; Christina Lipe, Treasurer; Jim Harris, Development Chairman; Mary Waggoner, Health, Education & Safety Chairwoman; Larry Cox, Zoning & Business Chairman; Lee Bailey, Beautification, Environment & Recreation Chairman; Bill Hutton, Historic Preservation Chairman; Emily Ellis, Board Director At Large; Nancy Lewis, Board Director At Large; Syvennia Smith, Board Director At Large; Helen Crawford, Board Director At Large.

Finally, I'd like to thank the many photographic contributors to the book, without whom the book would not be possible, including: Grady Amman, Barbara Asbury, Bob and Barbara Bailes, Lee Bailey, Joe Carroll Bell, Sam E. Bratton, Jr., Doris Bridges, Lorraine Burrows, Wanda Carter, Donnie Cathy, Cyndy Cox, Larry Cox, Harold Elkins, Wanda Epps, Vernon Hamilton, Chris Hoosier, Emma Jean Leek Huddleston, Harold Huffaker, Norma and Paul Kelley, Mary Helen Stephens Kirby, Kenneth Kermit Kitts, Mary Jean Laugherty Larison, Becky Lawson, Biddy Leahy, Elizabeth McCluskey, Johnny Lane McReynolds, Rubye McGhee, Ted Mitchell, Jennifer Montgomery, the McClung Historical Collection, Sue Newman, Carolyn Overton, Fletcher Reagan, Charles Reeves, Marsha Cox Robbins, Ruth Ann Rogers, Edna Mae Frances Scarborough, Mary Solomon, Bernice Stevens, Mercy Health Partners, the Tennessee State Museum, Katherine Cook Thomas, Burma Lawson Turner, Ethel Viles, Ann Watson, and Donna Watson.

If we have inadvertently left anyone out, you have our sincere and humble apologies. Unfortunately, some images could not be used because of their condition or format. If you have additional photographs of this or other areas of Knoxville that you would like to share, please contact the publisher, Park City Press, at 865-936-4533. We are a small imprint publisher of local history and genealogy, and are always interested in unique or custom projects.

www.ingramcontent.com/pod-product-compliance
Lightning Source LLC
Chambersburg PA
CBHW081136090426
42742CB00015BA/2857